The Ayatollah in the Cathedral

The
AYATOLLAH
in the
CATHEDRAL

MOORHEAD
KENNEDY

With an Afterword by Louisa Kennedy

A MYRIN BOOK

🎵 Hill and Wang   *New York*
A division of Farrar, Straus and Giroux

Copyright © 1986 by The Myrin Institute
Afterword copyright © 1986 by Louisa Kennedy
ALL RIGHTS RESERVED
First edition, 1986
Printed in the United States of America
Published simultaneously in Canada by
Collins Publishers, Toronto
Designed by Tina Kachele

Library of Congress Cataloging-in-Publication Data
Kennedy, Moorhead.
The Ayatollah in the cathedral.
"A Myrin book."
1. Iran Hostage Crisis, 1979–1981—Personal
narratives.   2. Kennedy, Moorhead.   3. Diplomats—
United States—Biography   I. Title.
E183.8.I55K43   1986   955'.054   86–11929

To my family, the outside hostages

ACKNOWLEDGMENTS

FOR MORE THAN FIVE YEARS, I have spoken to citizens' groups ranging from the Department of State to the American Legion to the pacifist Fellowship of Reconciliation, and to many religious groups, as well as educational institutions ranging from major universities to secondary schools, Masonic lodges and service organizations, patriotic societies, world-affairs councils, retirement homes, and clubs of all descriptions. To all my sponsors, and to the audiences whose questions prompted me to refine many of my ideas, I wish to express my gratitude.

This book began as a monograph, to be published by the Myrin Institute, whose Council for International Understanding I direct. Once it became clear that the monograph was not the appropriate format for this material as it had developed, the manuscript was shown to Hill and Wang, which accepted it for publication. To Marion and Olivia Gilliam, president and administrative director of the Myrin Institute, and to my editor, Arthur Wang, my appreciation.

For other help, I would like to thank my former hostage roommate, Frederick L. (Rick) Kupke, whose written record of his experiences in captivity along with my own was confiscated by our captors. Following our return, I dictated my recollections and had them transcribed, including certain episodes remembered from Rick's manuscript. To Dean George Packard, and the staff of the School of Advanced International Studies of Johns Hopkins University, to which the Department of State reassigned me after my return, and without whose cooperation this source material would not have been preserved, my thanks. Also to Mary Miller and the National Committee of the Episcopal Peace Fellowship, for dialogue; Trinity Church in New York, especially the Reverend John M. Palmer III; the Chautauqua Institution, under whose auspices, in July 1984, I delivered the lectures on which part of this book is based; Nicholas L. King, director of the Foreign Press Center of the United States Information Agency in New York; the Department of Church and Society of the Lutheran Church in America, and especially the Reverend George Brand; the Reverend Charles Cesaretti, formerly Public Issues Officer of the Episcopal Church Center; Brother Austin David, formerly Director of Studies of the Pope Paul II Center of Prayer and Study for Peace; Henry R. Geyelin; the Reverend Allan M. Parrent for useful theological terminology; the Albert and Anita Ehinger Foundation; Merloyd Lawrence, Dr. Cynthia M. Parker, Nicola DiToro, Janeth Thoron, and Edwin Hymovitz, for editorial assistance; Mrs. Donald Arthur and her friends in Huntington, Long Island, and many others around the country who contributed valuable editorial suggestions; Natasha Lutov for her typing and support.

Permission to quote from *American Hostages in Iran: The Conduct of a Crisis*, by Warren Christopher et al., under the editorial direction of Paul H. Kreisberg (New Haven: Yale University Press, 1985), is gratefully acknowledged. Also quotations from: ABC News, show 899 of Nov. 1, 1984; "What the Russians Really Want," by Marshall D. Schulman, *Har-*

per's, April 1984; *Reflections* (Diocese of New York, Region Two), March 1982; *Trinity News*, vol. 30, no. 5 (Dec. 1983); *The Worldly Philosophers*, by Robert Heilbronner (New York: Clarion Press / Simon and Schuster, 1953); Derek Bok, *The New York Times*, April 22–23, 1983; *The World War and American Isolation 1914–17*, by Ernest R. May (Cambridge: Harvard University Press, 1959); George Kennan, *The New Yorker*, Feb. 27, 1984; "But What About the Russians," by John E. Mack, *Harvard*, March–April 1982; *Terrorism, Threat, Reality, Response*, by Robert Kupperman and Darrell Trent (Stanford: Hoover Institution Press, 1979); *Arafat: Terrorist or Peacemaker?* by Alan Hart (London: Sidgwick & Jackson Ltd., 1985); *The Miami Herald*, June 30, 1985.

CONTENTS

The Ayatollah in the Cathedral

1 / TAKEOVER

SUNDAY STARTS THE Muslim workweek. On Sunday, November 4, 1979, I had planned, after an early staff meeting at the Embassy, to go straight downtown for a ten o'clock meeting with an Iranian banker. But he had called to suggest lunch instead, and so around 10:30 I was at my desk on the ground floor of the Chancery, the Embassy's office building, when a Marine came running down the hall. "Everybody downstairs. There's a break-in."

I looked out the window. A flood of young Iranian men, bunched together and carrying staves, were pouring through the open gate of the Embassy compound, heading for the Chancery. Some of them, their faces upturned, looked almost ecstatic, evidently hoping the Marines inside the building would shoot and make them martyrs. I told my staff and the visitors to the economic section to move fast. "But the safes"— Kathy Gross, my secretary, was horrified. "They're open." "Leave them," I said. "*Move.*" Kathy rolled her eyes. We moved quickly down to the basement, but almost immediately the students began to break in there, so we went up to the second floor, where a steel door promised safety.

Through the high picture windows in the chargé's office we could see a line of women students holding up a long banner for us to read. "We don't want to inconvenience you," the banner read. "We just want a set-in." No weapons were in evidence. Al Golacinski, our security officer, was being paraded around, arms tied behind his back. Well, I thought, I won't be getting any more security violations.

It was hard, not being able to do anything. Ann Swift, a political officer, and Colonel Charles Scott, of the military mission, were manning the telephones. Many of us busied ourselves looking out the windows and relaying information to Swift, who was talking to the Department of State in Washington; Scott was in touch with the chargé, Bruce Laingen, at the Foreign Ministry. Aside from one senior officer, everyone remained calm. He was frightened to death, his eyes glazed, and he wandered about aimlessly. I fretted about the Iranian banker. How could I make lunch? With the telephones tied up, how could I get word to him?

With no one formally in charge, decisions were made by consensus. When the students started banging on the steel door, we moved a table to block it and piled chairs on top of the table. The students demanded a negotiator. We dismantled the barricade, and John Limbert, a political officer whose Farsi was fluent, was slipped through the half-opened door. We closed the door and rebuilt the barricade.

Smoke began to seep under the steel door. Were they going to burn us out? On the other side of the door, Golacinski, our captured security officer, urged us to surrender. "They won't hurt you. Let them do their thing. Delay will get you nowhere."

Somebody shouted back at him, through the door, that someone in the Foreign Ministry was trying to contact Khomeini, Iran's religious leader. "Fuck that," he shouted. "Open the door." And so we dismantled the barricade for the second time and let the students in.

The students went about their task quickly and calmly. Told to form a line, we gave each other stick-with-it smiles. I caught the eyes of my two Iranian secretaries and smiled at them. They smiled back. Someone said, "They're tying us up." We were blindfolded, our hands tied, and then we were led down to the main floor. "Step down," my student escort told me. "Turn right." As we went down the stairs, he kept repeating, "Vietnam, Vietnam."

We were led outside the Chancery and then on to the Residence five minutes away. On our way, we heard patriotic singing; from the sound of the voices, they were women. At the Residence, I was tied to a chair. When my blindfold was removed, I found myself in a small room. In the chair next to me, also tied, sat a CIA officer. "You realize," he said, "that we're hostages." Somehow I could not take it in. The most the students would do, I thought, was set fire to the Chancery. I was, foolishly, still worried about lunch with the Iranian banker.

Then we were moved into a bigger room, to join a larger group of hostages. The students seemed perplexed, unsure of themselves, as if, having done what they set out to do, they had no idea what to do next. For our part, we began testing them for limits, trying to see how strict they were going to be. I led my colleagues in whistling "Rally Round the Flag." When one student asked for the keys to all private cars, I lectured him on the sanctity of private property. At another point, I marched off to the bathroom without asking permission. A student ran after me. "Excuse me, sir, you must ask permission." The women hostages were led through. I grinned at Kathy as she passed by. "Keep smiling."

That night I spent on the floor of a room with French doors

leading to the patio. Our guards were still very unsure, and escape, at moments when they were not in evidence, looked easy. My CIA colleague and I decided that going along with our captors, for what we still thought would be a detention of short duration, was the wiser course.

The next morning the students, determined to show us who was boss, marched us into the main reception room of the Residence, made us sit facing the wall, and blindfolded us and tied our hands behind our backs. I could see down, under the blindfold. My green polka-dot tie and the Oriental rug on the floor became links with reality. From sheer discomfort, I crinkled my nose, and the blindfold began to slip down, my links slowly disappearing. At that point, I nearly cried in panic. I soon discovered that every time I was taken to the bathroom, a guard would retie my blindfold, which once again would start its slow progress down my nose. And with all this going on, I developed a new worry. I was expected that evening at a dinner party, to be given by an Iranian lady I had only just met. How would I get word to her?

As night fell, the students relaxed their security measures. They untied my hands from the back of the chair and retied them to the arms; I was far more comfortable. After supper, they took my blindfold off, and I was allowed to sleep on the floor. Later that night, a student woke me and some others and, addressing me courteously by name, asked me to accompany him. From the few questions student guards had asked me earlier about my position in the Embassy and where my office was, it was clear that they were trying to identify the CIA people. Prepared only for a formal interrogation over at the Chancery, I found myself with a blanket over my head, loaded with two other hostages into a van, and driven off into the night. "I hear," one of them whispered, "they wasted two Marines."

Even when I heard weapons being loaded into the back of the van, it did not seem possible that the same thing could happen to me. Remembering a spy movie I had once seen, I tried to memorize the turns of the van, but it drove on and on, and I very quickly lost all sense of our direction. We ended up in a house where my watch was taken without my knowing it (I was still blindfolded). I was led upstairs with the others, and my blanket removed.

Three of us found ourselves in a small bedroom with a double bed. Our hands remained tied, loosely enough, however, so that we could slip in and out of our bindings. "Don't you want to take your jacket off?" one of my new bedfellows whispered in some curiosity. Along with my necktie, I had kept it on for more than thirty-six hours. I slipped out of my bindings and removed my jacket and necktie. Keeping them on had served its purpose. They had reassured me, and I imagined they had influenced my captors—one does not hold an American diplomat hostage, not for long. Taking them off marked the end of hours of denial. I slowly began to accept, and face, the fearful implications of my new situation. As I drifted off to sleep, I could hear through the window a lone voice singing. This was the beginning of Muharram, the season when Iranians remember the martyrdom of Husain, grandson of the Prophet, for whom this beautiful melody was a lament.

2 / EXPELLING
THE WEST

FIVE AND A HALF years later, in June 1985, sound asleep at two in the morning, I screamed "Help!" My wife, Louisa, woke me and quieted me down. My heart still pounding, I realized that my worst hostage nightmare, that they were coming to take me away to be executed, was with me again after several years' absence. Two weeks before, passengers on TWA flight 847 had been taken by Lebanese Shiites and were being held hostage. The television networks, remembering my considerable experience before the cameras following my release, approached me to explain to the American public the inner feelings of a hostage at various stages of captivity. With two or three interviews a day, I was reliving my 444 days of captivity far too vividly for my own good.

So, in its way, was the American public, as it responded to the hijacking of TWA 847 much as it had to the Iranian crisis. Following a prescribed ritual, families wrapped yellow ribbons around the nearest tree, and, to anyone who showed up with a camera crew, confided their feelings, such as their religious beliefs, which Americans do not usually impart even to close friends. All this conveyed bewilderment, and a need for reassurance in the face of developments utterly at variance with their view of America's position in the world. Other, less worthy feelings, also surfaced. Americans who should have known better, including our Chief Executive, trumpeted ethnic slurs about Middle Easterners which, if directed at any group in our polyethnic society, would not be acceptable. Primal emotions surfaced; some called for revenge, contemplating mass destruction of innocent Lebanese. Incensed over this episode of emerging international violence, America ignored its own tacit acceptance of a high degree of domestic violence, not to mention violence as a staple in our television entertainment.

TWA 847 provided Americans with the opportunity to ascribe to others what they least liked about themselves. Their outrage likewise reflected fear and uncertainty. Illusions of American invulnerability, based on assumptions of unquestioned American strength, had been upset again, this time by young Muslims prepared to die for their cause.

After the Tehran hostages came home, the American people, and the United States government, preferred to think that their imprisonment and the nation's nagging self-doubts could safely be put behind them. Hence the closing rituals, the parades to welcome home the returning hostages, my own collection of keys to various cities, the awards. By making instant heroes of those who were merely lucky to have survived, we converted what had been perceived as a national humiliation into a victory. This crisis over, never to be repeated, the American people could shift their attention to more agreeable matters. Then came the demolition of not one but two American embassy chanceries in Beirut by Shiite fanatics, and the blowing up, with horrifying casualties, of a Marine barracks. After the TWA affair and then the taking of an Italian cruise liner, the hijacking of an Egyptian airliner, and the massacres in the Rome and Vienna airports, the public realized finally that the Iranian takeover was not an aberration to be closed out with parades but the precursor of a mounting wave of Middle East terrorist reaction against the United States.

A point on which confusion often arises, and which should be clarified at the outset, is what *kind* of terrorism is meant. As the TWA crisis erupted, the news media discussed Italy's Red Brigades, Baader-Meinhof, and other manifestations of international terrorism, lumping them all together. Terrorism is indeed an international conspiracy in the sense that connections between terrorist groups are strong, especially in the matter of training. Terrorist groups, however, differ widely in their motivation, and that is what should concern us most. Unless and until we understand why young men and women are willing to put their lives at risk, we will not begin to address the problem. Dr. Franco Ferracuti, professor of forensic psychiatry at the University of Rome, and former adviser on terrorism to the Italian Ministry of the Interior, lists five types of motivation: (1) resistance to colonial rule; (2) ethnic separation (i.e., Basques, Corsicans, Puerto Ricans); (3) internal political factors; (4) support for external takeover (i.e., Vietnam); (5) ideological belief.

The principal ingredients of Middle East terrorism are (1) and (5)—it is Middle East post-colonial religious and national terrorism. Ideology, the motivation of anarchism in the nineteenth century, now means a combination of nationalism and religion, sometimes with a leavening of Marxist vocabulary. And "colonial" means post-colonial, the continuing impact of the West on the Middle East, following the withdrawal of the West's mandates, protectorates, and other forms of political rule, direct or indirect. The exception is Israel, which, with its strong American support, represents in the eyes of its Arab enemies the political colonialism elsewhere expelled from the Middle East. Political colonialism, in Arab eyes, returns intermittently in such forms as the American military interventions in Lebanon in the early 1980s. Middle East terrorism finally succeeded in forcing the withdrawal of the United States Marines, with their naval support, in February 1984.

More important, the impact of the West, against which terrorism is a reaction, takes the form of commercial and psychological and cultural penetration. The reaction is all the more violent because of feelings of powerlessness within their own society as well as against the dominant West. Frustration, from lack of sexual and economic opportunity, heightens the reaction still further, and leads directly to violence.

Less obvious, perhaps, as causes of terrorism, are the self-confidence and asserted superiority of the dominant Western-ers. Our very success brings out feelings of inferiority and resentment. And when the United States fails to live up to its pretensions, and to Middle East expectations, the reaction is one of anger and disappointment. Middle East terrorism is a reaction against the colonialism which in effect said that since the Middle East needs the West to govern it properly, its institutions and values, except to the extent that we, their governors, have to work within them, are of no particular consequence. The terrorist reaction is a statement of identity, a demand that the post-colonial Middle East, its people, val-ues, and institutions, be taken seriously by the West, and particularly by the United States.

On November 1, 1984, the fifth anniversary of the takeover of the U.S. Embassy in Tehran, ABC television's "Nightline" brought me face to face once again with Hossein Sheik-holeslam, today a Deputy Foreign Minister of Iran, and re-portedly the coordinator of Iranian-inspired terrorism in other countries, including Lebanon. When I first met him, in Feb-ruary 1980, in the cramped basement room of the Chancery, the Embassy office building where three of us were confined, he had noted a certain constraint in the conversation. "We can-not talk freely," he said, "with me as a captor and you as cap-tive. Perhaps, after this is all over, we can meet somewhere and talk freely." Now, via satellite, I asked him what he had hoped to accomplish by taking over the Embassy in Tehran. He replied that when he was a student in the United States most of the American people did not know where Iran was. "Right now . . . most of the American people know where Iran is." Making Americans aware that Iranians exist, that they have an identity worthy at least of notice, justified in his view the attention-getting device of an embassy takeover. A number of passengers on the hijacked TWA 847 did not know where Beirut was, much less about Lebanon's Shiites. That knowledge gap was also filled, not just for the passengers but for the entire American people.

On that same ABC broadcast, he went on: "More importantly, they [i.e., the Americans] know what Iran says and what Iran stands for—Eastern, not Western." Iran not only exists, then, but it stands for its own values, not ours. Iran expected to be judged by those values, not by those of the West, which it had rejected.

My basement conversation with Sheikholeslam in 1980 afforded me other glimpses of the motivation of the Middle East terrorist. His group, I reminded him, was holding us "contrary to international law." He replied, scornfully: "And what is international law but the rules by which you, the powerful industrial states, justify what you do to poor developing countries like Iran?" His revolution rejected all that we stood for. And Sheikholeslam added: "Besides, you do not observe them yourself." He was referring, of course, to our Embassy's infractions of international law—the Belgian and West German passports with pictures of CIA officers but bearing other names, and the forged Iranian entry stamps which our captors uncovered when they took over our files.

These were minor details, and we said so. But five years later, and in a larger sense, he might well have been referring to TWA 847. Until that hijacking brought them to the nation's attention, how many Americans were aware that Israel was holding more than seven hundred Lebanese, primarily Shiites, in defiance of international law? To paraphrase Sheikholeslam, the United States had one rule for those holding Americans illegally, another for those who hold Arabs illegally. Not only did TWA 847 invoke a special grievance but also the failure of the United States to live up to a precept of which it is justly proud, of equal treatment under law. This is a classic example of the high expectations / deep disappointments syndrome of which more than fifty of us in the Embassy in Tehran fell victim.

Middle East terrorists, as I have experienced them, do not look to the Soviet Union with high expectations, so there is no consequent disappointment. I remember asking one of my guards in Tehran why, in view of the Soviet invasion of Afghanistan, his government was prepared to antagonize the United States. "Suppose they do to Iran what they are doing to Afghanistan?" He replied, "The Soviets are a danger, but you are the *real* danger." If the Soviets were the real danger, it would be their diplomatic establishment and civil airlines which would be the primary target of terrorist attack, rather than our own. The difference does not lie in a greater readiness by the Soviets to retaliate. Their diplomats have been taken hostage and even murdered, and the Soviets did not retaliate, at least not militarily.

The difference between the terrorist targeting of Americans over Soviets is hard for Americans to understand. We are brought up to believe that the Soviets are "bad," whereas we are "good." That to many we are the enemy demands more self-recognition than Americans are prepared for. Why this is so, and how and why we Americans must understand this, is a basic theme of this book. In a sense, the Muslims are holding a mirror up to us, in which we may see ourselves as they see us. The image is not always agreeable. Yet we must contemplate it, if we are to deal effectively with the Middle East and the terrorism by which its young activists are making their presence felt.

My experience with the Middle East began long before I joined the Foreign Service in 1960. As early as 1946, at Groton School, I drew the negative side in a debate, "Resolved, that Palestine should be made a Jewish state." The judges, headed by a returning graduate, McGeorge Bundy, after commending me for my rebuttal, decided that the affirmative had presented the better case. I was angered by my defeat and researched the subject further, writing to the Zionist Organization of America and the newly established Arab Office in Washington, D.C. Finally, I wrote a paper entitled "The Problem of Palestine," which won the history essay prize. In 1967, during the six-day Arab–Israeli war, while assigned to our embassy in Beirut, I lent a copy of my school essay to the political section. It had held up very well.

I entered Princeton in 1948, and began to study Arabic, the first freshman in the country to do so. My senior thesis, on the origins and development of French colonial theory with respect to Algeria in the mid-nineteenth century, was my first effort to come to terms with how the West approaches the Middle East. The French view of the Arabs, I discovered, was divided. Under the monarchy and the Second Empire, Army officers were in the ascendant. Generally of aristocratic background, they were sympathetic to the Arabs, whom they had conquered, and saw in the religious and hierarchical Arab society the kind of old regime they would like to have retained in France. They projected their French backgrounds and aspirations onto the North African scene, and looked forward to a feudal Franco–Arab dominion under French rule. However, the French colonists, of lower social status and republican in sympathy, aspired to create new lives for themselves in an

Algeria which they wanted to be wholly French in character. The fall of the Second Empire and the establishment of the Third Republic in 1871 ensured that the colonists' view prevailed, and Algeria became an extension of France, until in the mid-1950s the native Algerians expelled the French. The Algerians became role models for my Iranian captors, determined to expel from Iran what the West represented.

Between my sophomore and junior years at Princeton, in the summer of 1950, I visited Iran for the first time, traveling with a water-well driller from Tabriz in the northwest to Shiraz in the south. I ate onions in the shade of village archways, and in many other ways gained a glimpse of the magic of Iran which captivity could never dispel. I also had my first glimpse of resentment against the West. Only nine years before, in 1941, the British in concert with the Soviets had invaded Iran. Their excuse was alleged, but never proven, pro-German sympathies on the part of Reza Shah Pahlavi. They deposed Reza Shah, putting in his place his son Mohammed Reza Shah, the Shah, as he was known to the American public. During my travels through Iran, I listened to a young man describe the British invasion of 1941 and I knew how humiliating it must have been.

British influence in Iran was still strong in 1950, giving rise to a quasi-colonial relationship. The British regarded Iran as a source of oil, for which they paid ridiculously small royalties, and as a captive market for their exports. "I'm sorry," a senior British official told the senior American adviser to the Iranian government, with whom I was staying, "but these people will buy *British* locomotives." The American adviser had just been pointing out that American locomotives, being diesel, were far better suited to the Iranian railways, with their many tunnels, than the British steam-driven engines. The Iranians ended up buying British.

As a young and quite naïve student, I was horrified at this naked exercise of power. How long, I wondered, would the Iranians stand for it? One year later, I was fascinated to read that the British oil holdings had been nationalized. A *Life* photograph remains in my mind—of a British cruiser standing by to cover the evacuation of the personnel of the Anglo-Iranian Oil Company (today British Petroleum). It was clear that the cruiser was powerless to do anything but provide transport. It never occurred to me then that America would also undergo expulsion and humiliation at the hands of a successor revolution, in retribution for the role of dominant power which we had taken over from the expelled British and exercised for twenty-five years.

At Princeton, I developed an interest in theology, which has remained with me. Its foundation was perhaps laid a little earlier, at Groton, where, as something of a rebel, I resisted the school's strong religious indoctrination. Fortunately, my mother was Unitarian, which gave me an excuse. To the examination question "What is the significance of the Incarnation?" I replied, "There is no significance to the Incarnation." The school made things very clear, however. I did not have to believe the answer, but I had to write it down. In self-defense, then, I became an amateur theologian. And at Princeton, in my junior year, I became interested in Byzantine church history. My paper, "Papal Intervention in the Monophysite Controversy," with its patriarchs battling over the formulation of church dogma, proved an excellent preparation for my later experience with warring American ambassadors, each trying to outshine and sometimes shoot down the others in telegrams, and so impose his views on the formulation of American foreign policy. And, unlike most of my future colleagues in the Foreign Service, I was always aware of the dynamic role that religion plays in foreign affairs.

Following my graduation from Princeton in 1952, I entered

the Army and was sent to Europe. I saved up my leave and in the winter of 1954 visited North Africa. I organized a small caravan to cross first the desert and then the high stony plateau between Touggourt and Guerrara in the Algerian Mzab. Relations with my camel were never the best, but stopping at water holes where caravan trails intersected, and listening to the gossip of the desert, was paradise. After being discharged from the Army at Camp Kilmer in New Jersey in the autumn of 1954, I returned to my parents' home in New York, and there, on my first evening out as a civilian, I met Louisa. I proposed to her that very evening, and we were married in June 1955. Louisa was a drama major at Sarah Lawrence, where she was developing talents that stood us well throughout our service together abroad. Always a leader, she helped in 1979 to rally the hostage families, whose spokeswoman she became. And she bore me four wonderful sons.

In 1955, I entered Harvard Law School, not because I wanted to be a lawyer, but to take advantage of the educational benefits of the Korean GI Bill, to which I was entitled. Bored to tears, I finally managed to specialize in Islamic law, which fascinated me. Shortly after graduation, a professor at the law school recommended me to *Collier's Encyclopedia*. Its 1983 edition still carries the article I wrote in 1960 entitled "Islamic Law," and I continue to lecture on this magnificent statement of man's duties to God and his fellow man. Midway through law school, in 1957–58, I took an academic year to pursue Arabic at MECAS, the Middle East Centre for Arab Studies, in Shimlan, Lebanon. The school, which was run by the British Foreign Office, would admit private students for a fee, and after several months as an independent student, I was formally admitted—the school's first enrolled American. My studies did not work out, because civil war erupted in Lebanon, and Shimlan, on the ridge in the Souf overlooking Beirut International Airport, was a strategic location.

This is not the book in which to analyze the causes of that conflict. It had much to do with Gamal Abdel Nasser, the Arab nationalist, and ruler of the United Arab Republic of Syria and Egypt, then at the height of his prestige after the fiasco in 1956 when the British and the French attempted to regain the Suez Canal. It had something to do with United States efforts to influence the Lebanese elections of 1956; those who felt cheated out of electoral victory took to the streets. It had much to do with Lebanese factors too complex or bizarre to detail here.

At noon one day in the spring of 1958, as Louisa and I were greeting our guests for a luncheon buffet, a man armed with a submachine gun appeared in our garden. He was of the PPS, the Syrian Popular Party, a private army which was moving in to occupy Shimlan. As Louisa was later quoted in the *Herald Tribune*: "But we decided to go ahead with the party anyway and it was a great success!" What we thought would be a local conflict in the mountains turned out to be far more serious, yet not without its baffling Lebanese paradoxes. Of the two protagonists, the PPS ideologically were dedicated to a Greater Syria and thus to the elimination of an independent Lebanon. Were they therefore not opposed to the official government of Lebanon? No—they supported it. Opposed to the PPS were the Druze, whose center at Mukhtara lay farther back in the Souf. Some weeks later, early in the morning, the director of the school, Donald (later Sir Donald) Maitland, received a letter from Kamal Jumblatt, the Druze leader. After reciting the favors bestowed by Queen Victoria on one of his ancestors, Jumblatt warned that his forces were about to attack the PPS forces in Shimlan. And so the student body, complete with wives and small children, fled Shimlan in a caravan of cars, white "nappies" flying to signal our neutrality. The caravan made its way down a donkey path to Souq el Gharb, where we took refuge behind the lines of the Lebanese

Army. As it turned out, the Druze attack failed; their troops ate some recently sprayed apples in the orchards outside the town and fell ill.

Louisa and I never returned to Shimlan, although we hoped to. In Beirut, a few weeks later, we met at the British Embassy with Donald Maitland, to discuss the possibility of a resumption of studies, when someone looked in. "We've had a report from IPC [the Iraq Petroleum Company]. Revolution in Baghdad." "Oh, poor Mr. Maitland," Louisa exclaimed. Iraq, where Maitland had long served, was almost the last major bulwark of British influence in the region. The loss of Iraq in 1958, following the nationalization of Britain's oil holdings in Iran in 1951 and disaster at Suez in 1956, marked the real end of Britain's moment in the Middle East. In response to the Iraqi revolution, the United States Marines landed in Lebanon. "Hey, lady," a Marine called out to Louisa from the turret of his tank, "where's the war?"

In captivity in Tehran more than twenty years later, I would think back on those days—on our youth and inexperience, and on the great events we had witnessed without fully understanding them. We had seen the changing of the guard. As the British moved out of the Middle East, the Americans had taken their place. Now, as a hostage, I realized that I was part of another changing of the guard, only this time the Americans were being ousted. Just as the British had placed so much trust in their man Nuri es-Said in Iraq only to see their influence eliminated by revolution, so we had made of the Shah "our man in the Middle East," with similar results. I recall how fellow students in Shimlan, mostly British Foreign Service, had been acutely aware that, for them, times were changing. I had run across an article, much underlined, in the school common room, "A New Role for Britain in the Middle East?" After a long period of power and control, it is, I thought, very hard to accept that your influence has waned, that you have lost your vital interests, that there is nothing you can do to regain your former eminence.

Shortly after my return from captivity, in 1981, I received a letter from a Lebanese friend, a Christian, suggesting that what had happened to me had had its origins at Suez, in the West's failure of nerve. Had the United States, my friend went on, only supported the British and the French, instead of opposing them, the West might have brought the Middle East once again to heel. No one would then have dared take over an American Embassy. My reaction was the same one I had had twenty-five years before. Military action in response to Egyptian nationalization of the Suez Canal in 1956, had it been followed through, might have restored that waterway temporarily to British and French control. But not for long. Military action could never restore Britain's prestige and influence. That would have necessitated not only a restoration of Britain's self-confidence and ascendancy but, more important, the acceptance by the people of the region of the legitimacy of Britain's role as the keeper of the peace. Once that role was no longer accepted, military use of force would not be perceived or accepted as a means to a legitimate end, but rather would be seen as the last lashing out of a dying empire.

The winding down of Britain's influence, as I witnessed it, may throw some light on the question of retaliation against present-day Middle East terrorism. Just as the legitimacy of Britain's role had to be accepted in order for Britain's power to be deployed successfully, so, too, the legitimacy of America's role as policeman in the Middle East would have to be accepted for military action to be justified in the eyes of those in the area whom we wished to influence. So long as military action is considered justifiable, then the inevitable civilian casualties, however regrettable, might also be accepted. We are dealing, however, with a Middle East in which important elements reject our leadership, and with it the legitimacy of the exercise of American power in the Middle East. Some of these elements have found ways, through terrorism, to make their rejection visible and felt. If America no longer exercises leadership in the Middle East, what would be the likely effect of retaliation against terrorists, retaliation that results in casualties and suffering among innocent civilians?

First, bombing civilian targets—as the Germans learned when they bombed London in 1940, or the United States when it bombed Hanoi in 1972—does not necessarily impose one's will. On the contrary, it tends to create solidarity and strengthen the others' resolve to resist. Second, in the Middle East, the use of force strengthens the perception of the United States as the enemy. It discredits our purposes, in their eyes, and deepens their hatred. Third, force arouses a desire for revenge. One of the hijackers of TWA 847 claimed that he had lost a wife and daughter to United States military action; the brutal murder of a United States Navy diver who was a passenger on that plane was not a coincidence. In the United States, there was little awareness that the shelling of Shiite settlements by the U.S. Navy in September 1983 had caused civilian casualties, until families of the victims were introduced to hostages taken on TWA 847, and their story relayed on television to the American public. And last, military retaliation creates martyrs. We gain nothing by giving fanatical Muslims what they want.

Louisa and I left Lebanon in July 1958, a few days after the Marines landed. We reclaimed Mark, our one-year-old son, from his grandparents in Maine, and I returned to law school, from which I was graduated in 1959. We moved to Washington, where our second son, Philip, was born, and I became a research analyst, a civil-service position, in the Bureau of Intelligence and Research (INR) in the Department of State. The job was a temporary one while I waited to pass the Foreign Service examinations. I entered the Foreign Service in March 1960, and after a refresher course in Arabic, I went abroad to my first post, the American Legation in Taiz, Yemen. I had just turned thirty. Louisa remained at home until the birth of our third son, Andrew, in March 1961. Leaving Andrew with his grandparents, Louisa joined me with Mark, aged three, and Philip, aged one, in Taiz. Andrew joined us the next year.

This was the old Yemen, still the Mutawakkilite Kingdom. Many stories could be told about this country of beautiful mountains and valleys, and its extraordinary ruler, the Imam Ahmad. Possessed of absolute authority, he was also graced with impressive vitality. After an attempted assassination, the Imam, with six bullets in him, was moved from Hodeida on the coast up to Taiz. When this relatively old man had recovered sufficiently to satisfy a member of his harem, salutes were fired from the castle. One morning, I was at the airport to meet the incoming Ethiopian Airlines plane, and spotting the Director of Civil Aviation, I went up to greet him. Although he was still in command at the airport, his walk had a curious shuffle: there were chains on his legs that the Imam made him wear as a mark of royal displeasure. And Louisa will never forget her first Yemeni tennis match, with the Ethiopian chargé. The court available to foreigners was also the execution ground; on the fence posts around it were impaled the heads of those who had opposed the Imam.

I lasted in Yemen seventeen out of my scheduled tour of twenty-four months, until May 1962; I was reassigned early because I was quite incompetent to do the job expected. Following the custom with junior officers in those days, I had been made administration officer, possibly the most complex job in any diplomatic establishment. Yemen's peculiar circumstances did not make "keeping everybody happy," the mark of a good administrative officer, any easier. The job required experience and rank, and I had neither.

For all my problems there, Yemen taught me an important lesson which Westerners too readily ignore: the difference between Westernization and modernization. Since the ideas and values that Westernization imparts, as well as the tools that modernization brings, come from the West, we tend to regard them as indistinguishable. A strong argument can be made that it is hard to have one without the other. One cannot, for example, run a factory (modernization) unless everyone shows up on time (Westernization). Traditional elements in the Middle East, however, believe that a separation is possible, that they can incorporate the tools of the West while rejecting its values. For all the variety of factors involved in recent terrorist episodes, they cannot be understood except in terms of this rejection. I witnessed this conflict for the first time in Yemen. To the Imam Ahmad, modernization was desirable. He kept his country well policed with the aid of short-wave radio. And foreign-aid missions, American and Chinese (PRC), were providing his kingdom with better roads. But he feared Westernization, the importation of Western ideas and values, for these would destabilize the monarchy and ultimately lead to its overthrow.

The Imam had selected a few young men of middle-class background to study abroad. One of them, Ahmad Mufarreh, was sent for by the Imam upon his return from Cairo and Paris, and was questioned closely about what he had learned. "You have learned many novel and interesting things," the Imam told him. "Now you will go to prison, so that you will forget some of them." After several years, Ahmad was released and brought before the Imam, who informed him that he was to be married. The bride was fourteen, and Ahmad did not see her face until after the wedding. When I knew Ahmad, he was French–English translator at the Foreign Ministry. He also moonlighted as my teacher of Arabic. Ahmad mentioned to me one day that he would like his wife, Laila, to meet some

Americans, so Louisa and I invited them for dinner. I shall never forget the moment she threw off her outer garment, which made her look like a World War I French tank. Out stepped a beautiful girl, only seventeen, reveling in her new freedom. Dinner went well, and they invited us to their home. But Ahmad told us later that he feared for the marriage, unless he could get her out of Yemen and expose her to Western culture. He had passed through a door into the West, and she had not, so there was a world he knew that she could not share.

Before my captivity, I assumed, like other Americans, that the Westernization of the Middle East was a matter of time, that Mrs. Mufarreh would be expected to catch up with her husband. The possibility that so many in the Middle East who were perfectly able to live and think as Westerners would ultimately react against the West did not enter my mind. But I had not pondered the lessons of a book to which I was first exposed at Princeton, in the graduate seminar on Ottoman history—Arnold J. Toynbee's 1924 work, *The Western Question in Greece and Turkey*. Toynbee had covered, for *The Manchester Guardian*, Greece's ill-fated attempt to annex western Turkey, and argued that the term "the Eastern Question," then popular among historians to summarize the disintegration of the Ottoman Empire in Europe, and which states would fall heir to its territories, was not really the operative one. It was the *Western* question we should be talking about—the impact of the West on the Middle East, or perhaps the enormous discrepancy in the impact the one had on the other.

To apply Toynbee's argument to the present: Unless the Middle Easterner can find a way to make the Westerner aware of his existence (through an oil embargo or the taking of hostages), the Westerner, and particularly the American, can live easily without such an awareness. Except for the Black

Muslims, a fringe group within the American black minority, Middle East culture has little impact on American life. In contrast, the West, and particularly American culture, has long had a powerful impact on Middle East life, penetrating every facet.

And this is what Hossein Sheikholeslam was referring to in our satellite conversation in 1984. In a deeper sense, the question was: Who are we?—to which Sheikholeslam answered: "Eastern, not Western." As the dominant source today of the dynamic Western culture to which the Middle East has long been trying to relate, we Americans understand only with difficulty the pangs about their own identity which the impact of our culture can generate in Arabs and Iranians. Those Americans who applauded the Westernizing efforts of the Shah had little notion of how his programs had disrupted lives at all levels of society. Many Iranians, disoriented, forced to think in new and strange ways, to perform unfamiliar tasks in accordance with unfamiliar norms, humiliated by their inadequacies as they tried to behave as Westerners, and disinclined to become proximate Westerners, second-class at best, sought above all for a renewed sense of their own identity. Many of them found it in fundamentalist religion, and the taking of American hostages marked the expulsion of the agent of their disorientation. The violence of that expulsion was a measure of the depth and effectiveness of Western penetration.

Seen in context, the taking of the TWA hostages was also a reaction to Western penetration. Even after the TWA passengers were released, other Lebanese Shiites continued to hold the hostages who had been taken before TWA 847 was hijacked. Almost all of them were on the cutting edge of American cultural penetration of the region. In addition to an Embassy officer, they have included the librarian of the American University of Beirut, the dean of its agricultural faculty, a missionary, the administrator of the American University Hospital, and the chief of the local Associated Press bureau. The local bureau chief of Cable News Network was also kidnapped and escaped; the acting president of the American University of Beirut and a missionary were kidnapped and released; and Malcolm Kerr, president of the American University (with whom I studied Arabic), was shot and killed.

Beyond the threat to their identity, Western cultural penetration has still another dimension. One of my roommates during our captivity pointed out, not for the first time, that our captors "want to take their country right back to the thirteenth century." By then thoroughly fed up with him, I shot back: "So what's so great about the twentieth?" This was hardly the kind of proposition my fellow hostages were in a mood to entertain, however. Had it been possible to pursue the matter, I would have questioned whether the course of events which produced the twentieth century, the last half of which has been America's century, necessarily represents progress. We have imposed our idea of "the good" on the Middle East. But if it is so "good," why are they so forceful in rejecting it? Perhaps it is because they have tried it and found it wanting, indeed harmful, in important respects. If we are to understand and come to terms with the factors that generate Middle East terrorism, we had better look into the mirror that terrorism holds up to us, for what it tells us not about the terrorists' shortcomings but about our own. Only if we are able to do something about our shortcomings can we hope to regain the respect and moral leadership we once enjoyed in the Middle East and in the rest of the Third World.

As a student and in my first assignment in the Foreign Service, I began to develop an idea of these cultural conflicts, which ultimately resulted in the takeover of our Embassy in Tehran. The takeover was also the result of severe institutional weaknesses in the United States Foreign Service, in which I had spent twenty-one years. In the course of the assignments which followed Yemen, diplomatic postings in Greece, Lebanon, and Chile, as well as in the Department of State, I began to question some of the assumptions under which I had to operate, problems to which, in my efforts to conform to the system, I had closed my eyes. In captivity, however, awaiting execution, and only too aware of the misjudgments that had led to the takeover of the Embassy, I could no longer ignore the flaws, any more than the strengths, of the system into which I had tried to fit for over twenty years. Captivity freed me of the necessity to think like a Foreign Service officer; it allowed me to question, rather than accept, what I could not change.

Captivity offered me the opportunity to review my life as a student of the Middle East and as an American diplomat. It was there that this book began. Anxious to keep us occupied, and impressed that I wanted to write a book, my guards provided me with writing materials. "Here, Mr. Kennedy," said one, "don't use a BIC pen. Let me get you a *good* one." I knew, of course, that my manuscript would be confiscated. I concentrated on major episodes, and on my conclusions, polishing and memorizing them in order to be able to reconstruct them following my release. That material forms the core of this book.

The following two chapters are about my experience in the Foreign Service, up to the moment when the Embassy came under siege. In them, I will discuss the parochial and defensive views of individual and collective responsibilities, the segmented vision, the distortions by which highly intelligent, well-trained, dedicated men and women too often misperceive what is going on under their very noses. All these factors led to what was the Pearl Harbor of the Foreign Service. The chapter after that deals with my captivity, how I experienced, directly and personally, the reaction to the West that I have just been discussing. When I had the time to reflect, I was compelled to confront not only these issues but myself and what I wanted to do with the rest of my life.

After we were released, it became clear that the Department of State, in its effort to cover up the misjudgments that led to the takeover of the Embassy, was determined not to draw the conclusions it should have from the Iranian experience. Nor should I have been surprised. Historically, the Foreign Service has never been willing to reform itself. Fundamental reforms have had to be imposed from the outside. Only the pressure of informed public opinion, I concluded, could bring about necessary changes in the conduct of American foreign policy. And so I retired from the Foreign Service, exchanging for the increasingly futile effort to work from within the system a new challenge of identifying and developing ways to influence that large amorphous thing called public opinion. What I have learned from my second career constitutes the second half of this book. As I soon discovered, some of the forces at work on public opinion, notably the peace movement and the church elements that support it, embody much the same strengths and weaknesses as the Foreign Service. Neither enjoys having its conventional wisdom challenged. For example, the skepticism I voiced about the now-defunct Nuclear Freeze in the job I had taken, after my retirement, at New York's Cathedral of St. John the Divine, did not help my position there and certainly contributed to its termination.

More significantly, I found that the misjudgments that paved the road to disaster at Tehran cannot be laid at the door of the Foreign Service alone. The Foreign Service is made up of Americans. We all need to grow up internationally, to mature in important ways if our nation is to address Middle East terrorism effectively, and to grow in other ways, too, in order to offer a foreign policy worthy of the best we represent. After dealing with American attitudes which impede the development of such a policy, I conclude with some modest but I think workable proposals for stimulating our international maturing.

3 / A CAREER IN THE
FOREIGN SERVICE

MY ETHIOPIAN DC-6 droned north through the night sky. Behind me was Yemen, my false start. Ahead lay Athens, where the Department, realizing that it had done me a disservice, was prepared to give me a second chance. Dreading my reception at a new post under what could hardly be called favorable auspices, I fought back a sinking feeling. Then I spied the first approach lights to Athens and knew that it would all work out.

Having started at the bottom, as a visa officer, I was assigned in the summer of 1963 to take temporary charge of Protection and Welfare, and a full-scale mini-crisis. The Greek military authorities, on the principle that all who are of Greek blood, whatever their passports, are subject to Greek law, were attempting to fill their conscription rolls by drafting Greek-Americans who were visiting Greece for the summer. "Can you help me?" a voice came over the telephone. "I am a U.S. citizen. I was born in Detroit. I am in chains. They are marching me through Piraeus . . ." With the support of the Ambassador, Henry R. Labouisse, who was widely respected in Athens, we were able to generate enough pressure through the Greek Foreign Ministry so that the Greek military revoked their order insofar as it affected American citizens.

None of this went unnoticed by my superiors, and in January 1964 I was given a much better job, in a unit affiliated with the political section, which dealt with base rights and other politico-military matters. Its chief, Alfred Vigderman, was a superb mentor, and under him, my career really began. First, however, in part because of my strong background in Ottoman history, I was drafted to help with the first of many Cyprus crises. There were exciting all-night stands in the code room as urgent messages poured in, and the wonderful feeling of being in on a highly complex issue. Resistance by the Greek majority on Cyprus had forced Britain to grant independence. The question was: For whom? A substantial Turkish minority on the island, backed by the Turkish government, which had seen other offshore islands pass into Greek hands, had blocked the union of the island with Greece. The shakiness of the compromise Republic of Cyprus, under the presidency of the wily Archbishop Makarios, coupled with the Turks' literal interpretation of earlier agreements, spelled trouble.

We in Athens were thoroughly imbued with the Greek point of view. At our Embassy in Ankara, the same thing was happening, but from the Turkish perspective. As a result, the American embassies in Athens and Ankara became proxies for their hosts in a battle of telegrams to command Washington's attention and policy. Unfortunately for us, the American Ambassador in Ankara, Raymond Hare, was a past master at telegraphic combat. "I see his little game," muttered Norbert Anschuetz, our Deputy Chief of Mission, his face set. "Why," exclaimed Ambassador Labouisse, clutching another missive from Raymond Hare, "he must have taken leave of his senses!" I made a modest contribution by preparing and circulating a memorandum analyzing (from the incoming messages) Ambassador Hare's thinking, the better for us to outwit him. But we could not. As a friend involved in Greek–Turkish affairs back in Washington later told me, "We watched Ankara's star rise, and Athens's fall."

Washington's seeming tilt toward Turkey did not endear us to our Greek hosts, particularly at that sensitive period in Greek–American relations. The United States AID program had terminated in 1962; the period in which Greece, after years of German occupation and civil war, had depended heavily on American assistance came to an end. American advisers had served in Greek ministries, filling in until Greeks could receive the training and develop the expertise they did not have available to them in the 1940s. And now that Greece was no longer beholden to the United States for economic assistance, the Greek government signaled to us that their willing cooperation could no longer be taken for granted. The Director of American Affairs for the Foreign Ministry, Alexander Xydis, a man of great charm and intellectual accomplishment, was picked for the job because, as he later admitted to me, he knew how to be abrasive with Americans. On another level of discourse, a mob, under careful police control, would periodically march up Vassilissis Sofias Avenue to the Embassy, chanting, *Ela, exo, Labwees.* "Come on out, Labouisse!"

The United States cannot please everyone. Diplomats are paid to take a certain amount of abuse and incur risks. What began to trouble me in Athens, however, was not that our policy, in Greek eyes, seemed pro-Turkish. Perhaps our interests in Turkey did outweigh those in Greece. Rather, I was concerned with how we had arrived at that policy, or at any policy. Disagreements will always crop up. Some will be deeply felt. But rather than resolve them by dialogue and consultation, too many of those who work for our government, at all levels, take a confrontational, combative approach.

Whether it is called bureaucratic infighting or "turf," it means substituting one's parochial point of view, in the Department or abroad, for the larger interest one is supposedly serving. This raises the question of who determines the national interest, in terms to which those on the working level can relate. In my experience, the definition is at best so broad that bureaucratic infighters have all the scope they need to take adversarial positions. At its worst is the kind of infighting carried on at the cabinet level. If cabinet officers cannot think and behave consensually, how can those on the working level, whose career advancement depends on how often they "win"?

This mind-set in its various manifestations is part of the overall human condition, but it is exacerbated by traits in our national character which make it difficult for Americans to manage an effective foreign policy. Let me state that I subscribed to this way of thinking wholeheartedly; I fought vigorously in defense of my series of little anthills as if truth existed nowhere else. And in my final post, in Tehran, I saw such parochialism almost blow the cover and lose the life of a CIA colleague.

Athens introduced me to another weakness in American policy management. Under Alfred Vigderman's direction, my principal duty had been to negotiate military base rights, and included demarches to the Foreign Ministry on matters that no one else in the Embassy was willing to touch. For example, on one occasion I was sent to secure permission for our military to install a highly classified electronic device which was virtually certain to be a nuclear target in the event of all-out war.

Many years later, I ran into Vigderman in Washington. After serving as Country Director for Greece in the Department, he had retired to teach at the Fletcher School of Law and Diplomacy at Tufts University. I asked him what he was doing in Washington, and he replied that he had been called out of retirement to help prepare to undo some of the agreements that we had negotiated. "The Colonels," in a military coup d'état in 1967, had taken over Greece. That regime had received the full support of the United States government, a position explained by, among other reasons, the need to protect our rights to military bases. After the Colonels had fallen from power in the wake of their folly in bringing on the Turkish invasion of Cyprus, the new democratic regime wanted to punish the United States for its support of the Colonels, and was threatening to cancel our previously negotiated rights. Today, under Prime Minister Andreas Papandreou, the future of our bases is still clouded.

Thinking back on all this during my captivity in Tehran, I wondered at how easily our government becomes locked into old patterns, pursuing policies and agreements which may be as transitory as the regimes we expect will honor them. The Shah, and all we expected from him, cost us our position in Iran. Similarly, our support of the Greek Colonels put at risk the very assets that our support was expected to preserve.

Athens introduced Louisa and me to another aspect of life in the Foreign Service, its curious insularity. Granted the danger of seeing events entirely from the point of view of one's host country, there is the far more common danger of not understanding the local point of view at all. Wherever we served, therefore, Louisa and I did our best to become part of the country and its life. The rewards were many, and the memories fond. But far too many of our colleagues, wherever we served, did not think such participation necessary. Seeing only other Americans required less effort. All they were interested in were "contacts," local people who would give them information. Nor did the Foreign Service rating system put much premium on how well one could enter into and understand a foreign society. Those who do, and there are many, are the more remarkable. But, by and large, America's isolationist traditions, combined with an unfortunate self-centeredness, keep too many of our Foreign Service officers aloof from the foreign environment they work in. Such psychological isolation can deprive their reporting of a sensitive dimension that is essential to general understanding. The problem arises even when they speak the local language.

My three-year assignment to Greece wound down in the spring of 1965. Louisa and I received orders for Lebanon, where we remained for the next four years, in some ways the best in our lives. How much those of us privileged to participate in Lebanese life gained by it! People remembered us from our student days, and Louisa, in her usual fashion, brought a wide variety of people into our lives. Even years later, Lebanese recalled our four years there: "You lived among us, as Lebanese . . ."

Instead of settling into an apartment, as most foreigners in Beirut did, we found a house near the American University, surrounded by a large garden. Caid the cook organized our lives, and Almoz the maid brought up our newborn son, Duncan. In the summer, we sent the three older boys to their loving grandparents on Mt. Desert Island, off the Maine coast. (And to this day, for all of them, Mt. Desert remains the family hearth.) Duncan spent the summer of 1968 with Almoz in her mountain village, where he became part of a typical extended Mediterranean family. When we returned to the United States in 1969, Duncan, by then four, was far more comfortable in Arabic than in English. He could also manage, his nursery school told us, quite good French, and even some Armenian.

Many Americans today, aware only of a Lebanon in constant civil strife, cannot imagine how tranquil it was. During our four years, only the Six-Day War, in July 1967, interrupted that tranquillity. Louisa and the boys, aged ten to two, were evacuated first. They spent the night at the American University, trying to sleep on the grass while flames from a burning oil tank lit the sky. At one point, Louisa heard a worried Lebanese security officer say that if the Muslim mob were to turn against the foreigners known to be in the university, there would be no way to hold them back. At the airport, the boys cheered as Pan American planes, as if in formation, swooped down one after another to carry off the evacuees. I was suffering from hepatitis and due to be evacuated too. But I agreed to manage and close down the evacuation center at the university if I could get on the last flight to Athens, where my family had gone. From Athens, we all went back to Maine, where I recovered my health, and at summer's end we returned to Beirut, where Caid and Almoz had everything ready for us. Like a bad dream, that foretaste of a grim future for Lebanon was soon forgotten.

Louisa introduced theater for children into Beirut, putting on a musical version of *Androcles and the Lion.* Muslim mothers, who clearly had never been in a theater in their lives, arrived with their curious and fascinated children. She also reviewed plays, put on in four languages, the rich offering of that most cosmopolitan of cities.

At the Embassy, I was the junior economic officer, with special responsibility for banking. Beirut had more than seventy banks. Not knowing the difference, when I arrived, between sight and time deposits, much less the French and Arabic terms for them, I had to learn fast. Fortunately, Arabs are born teachers, and I had a lot of help. But if busy bankers are to give you more than a single interview, you have to find ways to make it worth their while. They give only when they get. Quickly, I learned how to get along on the information circuit. You never ask a banker about his bank. After whetting his appetite with some juicy tidbit of banker's gossip, you ask about problems at somebody else's bank. I also learned about the 180° contacts, those who invariably told you the opposite of the truth, the direction of which you then obviously could plot.

Lebanese banks began to have trouble in 1966 when, with the rise in European interest rates, money from the Gulf began to be drained out of Beirut. Smaller banks soon started to fail. I had cultivated the bank inspectors and was able to report to Washington which banks were likely to fail and when.

Getting so deeply into Lebanon's volatile banking sector taught me much about the Lebanese people—their extraordinary individualism, and their optimism, born of centuries of having to live by their wits, that somehow everything would turn out all right. Sometimes it did not. Lebanon's largest bank, Intra Bank, survived on the dubious banking principle that it would cover its mounting short-term obligations through capital appreciation on such fixed assets as a French shipyard, an airline, and hotels and office buildings around the world. It was Intra's insolvency that precipitated Lebanon's banking crisis. More seriously from the American point of view, the United States Department of Agriculture held $21 million in Intra letters of credit. Joining with the governments of Lebanon, Qatar, and Kuwait in an effort to refloat the bank, the United States took shares in lieu of its claims, and for a considerable period—well into 1969, when the Department of Agriculture sent its permanent representative to Beirut—I represented my government on the new Intra board. It was an appallingly difficult job, made more difficult by my own government. While those of us in Beirut representing the U.S. government in its capacity as shareholder were trying to save the bank, the U.S. government at home, in its capacity as creditor, was helping itself to Intra's real estate in New York, in order to satisfy its claims.

Somehow I weathered that crisis. Indeed, the way I handled it seemed, briefly, to strengthen my influence. Then, through my own fault, I lost some of it. In negotiating a financial advisory contract with an American firm, I thought, American style, that I had authority from my colleagues on the board. They, Middle East style, had reserved the right to change their minds, and I felt I had had the rug pulled out from under me. Instead of accepting that on the board of a Lebanese bank I would have to act and think like a Middle Easterner, I got angry, coming across like a hateful, overbearing American. It was a learning experience I never forgot.

Others made their mistakes, too. The Ambassador, Dwight J. Porter, was, by his own definition, a "plunger," prepared to take any necessary risks. And helping to refloat the Intra Bank at a time when the Lebanese economy was doing badly, and when our reputation had fallen in Arab nationalist eyes after the Six-Day War, was certainly a positive gesture of friendship and support. What neither Porter nor I saw was the mire of Lebanese politics into which we were stumbling. Porter went a step further. Thinking that it was his prerogative as American Ambassador to pinpoint the next President of Lebanon, he picked Pierre Edde, Finance Minister at the time. Porter launched his "campaign" by taking Edde to lunch, in full view of "all Beirut," at the St. George Hotel. Lebanese friends noted that this kind of intervention by a foreign ambassador was no longer appropriate. What could I say?

The Lebanese government's shares in the refloated Intra Bank were held by the Ministry of Finance, and Lebanese board members reported to Edde. At one point, for solid reasons and in defense of my government's financial interests, I had to oppose my Lebanese colleagues on the board. They reported this to Edde, who, as the Ambassador's "nominee," was now in a position to raise hell at the Embassy. My immediate superior, the Economic Counselor, had to call Edde to apologize for the position I had taken. I drafted an angry memorandum—what a colleague, his eyes popping, called "the most extraordinary document I've ever seen"—and went

on leave to Morocco. In the memo, I blasted what I termed
the Marshall Plan mentality of senior officers who had entered
the service at a time when it was not only the right but the
duty of the United States to help shape internal developments
in other countries. Fortunately, my superiors held up the memorandum, and it never reached the Ambassador's desk. It
would have angered a kind, reasonable, and courageous ambassador, whom I liked and respected.

The Marshall Plan mentality is today a thing of the past.
Overreliance on personalities and particular groups remains a
problem, however. Sooner or later, there arises the need to
continue to support the person or group our government has
espoused, at a time when it is no longer convenient to do so.
It is not always easy to let go, as we saw with the Shah, whom
we had backed for more than thirty years, even restoring him
to power at one point. Or President Ferdinand Marcos in the
Philippines.

My assignment to Beirut came to an end as the summer of
1969 began. As part of my banking responsibilities, I had
come to know Elias Sarkis, then governor of the Central Bank
and later President of the Republic. Not long before Louisa
and I left for home leave and my first Washington assignment,
Sarkis invited us to his house in the foothills, and the cool of
the garden that was his passion. President Helou, he told us,
had entrusted him with dealing with the armed Palestinians
who had been expelled from Jordan and were being passed
onto Lebanon by the Syrians. "We push them back into Syria,"
Sarkis went on, "and the Syrians push them back on us. We
haven't the forces to maintain the integrity of our frontiers."
Later that week, Louisa and I attended a dinner party at
Desmond and Yvonne Cochrane's. She is a Sursok, from one
of the great Orthodox Christian families of Beirut, and her
Italianate palace, overlooking Ashrafiyeh, the Christian quar-
ter of East Beirut, was one of its landmarks. After dinner, as

we looked out from an upstairs balcony, I remarked to a friend, "You know, this is St. Petersburg, 1913."

Horror was soon to descend on Lebanon. The causes will be the subject of study and debate for years to come. Traditionally, the Lebanese government asserted that its troubles are the result not of civil war but of foreign intrusion, beginning with the Palestinians. But other factors cannot be ignored. Certainly, until 1975, when the fighting began, enormous oil-derived wealth poured into Lebanon, accentuating the differences between rich and poor. In 1969 I already had the suspicion, which my return in 1979 was to confirm, that it was the intrusion of this kind of wealth which activated the social unrest that is expressed in communal violence. During the early seventies, too, the vast influx of oil money into Iran, with its consequent conspicuous display and corruption, triggered discontent that in turn raised questions and kindled anxieties about Westernization. Indirectly, it helped generate the religious response that brought on the revolution and the hostage crisis.

My bank reporting had attracted some interest in the Economic and Business Bureau (EB) of the Department of State, and so in 1969, when I returned to Washington, the Bureau had already asked for my services. But banking problems are one thing, and theoretical economics are something else. I felt utterly lost among that elite group of trained Foreign Service economists, until the Bureau arranged for me to take the intensive six-month economics course at the Foreign Service Institute. The course was superb—it equips its graduates with at least the equivalent of an honors B.A. in economics—but economics, as a theoretical and predictive tool, never really interested me. To me, economics was useful to the extent that it helped one to understand the complex motives and behavior of people and nations. I had learned what was necessary, however, and supported by a very professional staff, I was able to handle what I feel was the most interesting challenge of my career. The Bureau asked me in November 1971 to set up the Office of Investment Affairs (OIA) and to be its first director. At long last, the Department was officially recognizing the multinational corporation as a major force on the international scene. The real reason for setting up the office, nonetheless, was more immediate—a foreign-policy mini-crisis leading to a highly divisive policy debate over what the United States response should be, a debate exacerbated by bureaucratic infighting between the Departments of State and Treasury.

Latin American governments had expropriated American private investments—primarily in mineral wealth and utilities —most of which had been established for a long time and had worn out their initial welcome. At the outset, they brought new jobs, promoted exports, earned foreign exchange, brought new knowledge, and in other ways stimulated the local economy. A generation or two later, those same private firms were not reinvesting their earnings. The outflow, in the form of interest, royalties, and dividends to the American shareholder, was perceived to be greatly exceeding any contribution the investment was making to the local economy. In many cases, this was certainly true. Aside from purely economic considerations, expropriation is not unlike the post-colonial terrorism we have been discussing—a reaction against dominant countries and cultures. Like terrorism, expropriation results from a complex of reasons. Canadians, for example, have uneasy feelings about Americans and other foreigners sitting in distant boardrooms making decisions which can affect vital Canadian interests and which Canadians can only with difficulty influence or prevent. In theory, the host government is sovereign and has the last word. In practice, it is not always easy to enforce national sovereignty, particularly for a weak Third World government, which may be susceptible to corruption and may not have access to sophisticated legal and accounting methods.

More important, foreign investment is usually accompanied by foreign ideas, foreign tastes and standards. Expatriate American business communities (as well as many but not all Foreign Service people) generally live and act as if "the locals" hardly exist. Such Americans, Louisa and I saw, tend to set their wagons in a circle. A few token locals, at most, are allowed to climb over the traces and join the American campfire, to talk of American things. A large American business community with living standards far more opulent than those of the host community can arouse deep anti-American feelings. Such factors contributed materially to our debacle in Iran.

Neither post-colonial terrorism nor expropriation can be addressed without an understanding of the complex motives of those who practice them. When in 1971 I tried to explain to a U.S. Treasury official why a host government felt impelled to expropriate an American company, he retorted accusingly, "You are arguing *their* side." I had to respond to the same kind of accusation when I came home from Iran and explained to lecture audiences why our student captors felt they had to take over the Embassy. Those who think in terms of "us" versus "them" fail to understand that what is at stake is not a battle but a series of relationships. When terrorism or expropriation surface, something in those relationships has gone sour, and our captors in Tehran were more aware of it than we.

In lectures and briefing sessions in 1972–74, I used to point out that the investment relationship is not unlike marriage. It, too, begins with a honeymoon. It, too, goes through almost predictable periods of strain. Nearly all countries have problems with investment, whether they are investors in other countries or are themselves invested in. With Latin American groups visiting Washington, I used to cite the example of "reverse investment," foreign investment in the United States. After the Japanese started to invest in the U.S. and they began to make their presence felt, an abundance of mail came to the Department: "Who won the war, anyway?" "To think that the flag we love, for which we fought and died, which has flown so proudly over our country, is to be replaced by the Rising Sun!" My deputy, Clarke Ellis (today director of OIA), established a file for this correspondence labeled "Pearl Harbor II."

Foreign investment is a major test of whether peoples of different cultures can live and work together on the basis of perceived common benefits, reconciling differences as they arise. For if the parties, investor and host government both, are not aware from the beginning of the need for agreed changes in the terms of the relationship as it evolves, then the investment relationship sooner or later will run into trouble. By 1971, such relationships were failing all over Latin America. Outraged American investors were demanding compensation or that something be done to protect their interests. In Latin America, pressures to end what many local governments saw as foreign exploitation were building up. The first reaction of the United States was confrontational and punitive. It took the form of sanctions—the withholding of United States development assistance, or voting against assistance contemplated by international lending agencies. In justification, the United States and the World Bank argued that countries that expropriate without at least paying compensation in accordance with the norms of international law are discouraging foreign investment, thus undercutting their own prospects for development.

What was forgotten then, and is today in the case of terrorism, is that public browbeating of others, while useful for domestic consumption, does not always yield positive results. Nor does it rebuild a relationship gone sour; it will not get North Americans once again to want to invest, or Latin Americans to accept such investments. The most successful settlement of an expropriation during those years, of the International Petroleum Company in Peru, was made possible only because negotiations, conducted by the Departments of State and Treasury together, took place in secret. And while official Washington generally trumpeted its indignation and moralized over the undoubtedly adverse effects of expropriation on the host country's economic development, we in the Office of Investment Affairs saw examples of American companies writing their losses off—with considerable tax benefits—and then quietly negotiating new relationships with the same governments.

In the policy debates over how to respond to expropriation, Treasury supported a hard-line, automatic response; State took a more flexible approach. The issue was first joined over a public statement on expropriation. Later, controversy continued over how and when to apply sanctions. Underlying these conceptual differences was an effort by Treasury to strengthen and expand its international jurisdiction. (Similarly, in responding to Middle East terrorism, the hard-liner, pursuing a single-issue approach, has an initial advantage in a policy debate over those whose approach embodies more than one issue, or who see that another side exists.) Unlike the Department of State, which has responsibility for the whole array of foreign-affairs issues, Treasury could afford the hard-line, single-issue approach. Its Secretary, John Connally, found it easy to take advantage of State's reluctance to sacrifice all our Latin American interests for this one. It was, he said, a reluctance to support American business. And in a business-oriented Nixon Administration, this allegation carried weight.

Word of these bureaucratic battles began to spread. A bemused British Embassy began to report on them. As a young British Treasury attaché noted over lunch at La Niçoise, at Her Majesty's Government's expense: "Mind you, we have our bureaucratic squabbles, too, but perhaps not pursued with quite the same, ah, vigor." A Ph.D. dissertation on such squabbles, written as they were finally winding down, awarded us at State higher marks for bureaucratic infighting than those at Treasury. Some years later, at a meeting with one of my erstwhile Treasury opponents who subsequently returned to academic life, we both deplored the time and energy wasted in this fighting. How much might we have accomplished if we had tried to work together!

The years 1971–72 were also a period of detente with the Soviet Union, which had a strong economic, as well as political and military, component. The economic key was to be the grant to the Soviet Union of most-favored-nation status on tariffs. For that, the Soviets were willing to settle their long-pending lend-lease account on terms equal with other World War II lend-lease recipients. We all knew that the Soviets had little to sell us. Their goal was psychological—international recognition that they were entitled to export goods to us on the same basis as others. We were keenly aware of Soviet sensitivity to discrimination, to the stereotype that they were somehow our cultural and technological inferiors. The Soviets also knew that we liked to collect old debts.

The priorities of the detente negotiations were set forth by Henry Kissinger. At a large inter-agency meeting at the Department, I watched him reject the order of interests that we on the economic side of State had advanced. Political objectives were to take precedence. Feeling somewhat let down by the lower status accorded my parochial interests, I was nevertheless relieved that someone was reconciling the myriad demands of the bureaucracy. But bureaucratic battles lay ahead, this time with the Department of Commerce. Under its ambitious secretary, Peter G. Peterson, Commerce wanted to monopolize the economic side of the detente process, and thus gain hegemony over future economic relations with Eastern Europe. Unfortunately for Commerce, the settlement of international debts, the key to the trade negotiations, was by law entrusted to the Department of State. Within the Department, it was the responsibility of the Economic and Business Bureau, and within that, the Office of Investment Affairs. Hence I found myself at Washington National Airport greeting Vladimir Alkhimov, the Soviet Deputy Minister of Foreign Trade and chairman of the Soviet team. Our chairman was Assistant Secretary of State Willis C. Armstrong, and I was his deputy.

Our negotiating symmetry with the Soviets was perfect. Each wanted what the other had to give. And as the two teams got to know each other, we were able to work out a debt-settlement package that we could jointly sell to Washington and to Moscow. Much of the credit for this cooperative atmosphere went to Mr. Alkhimov, and he seemed to recognize in me an equally strong desire to make the negotiations a success. "Mr. Kennedy has shown creative imagination in helping us with past problems," Mr. Alkhimov said at a difficult moment. "He will again show creative imagination in helping us with this problem!"

We were fortunate, too, in the relationship that had been developed by President Nixon and Donald Kendall, chairman of Pepsi-Cola, when Nixon was a lawyer for that company. Part of the not so hidden agenda of those trade negotiations, for which the lend-lease negotiations were the threshold, was Pepsi's bid for a monopoly of cola drinks in the Soviet Union, in return, we assumed, for marketing Stolichnaya vodka in the United States. Kendall, who became a kind of godfather to the lend-lease negotiations, invited our Soviet counterparts to stay at his country place in Greenwich. They seemed to have other high-level contacts as well. I recall some of their delegation coming to me to request permission to visit Florida. "Oh," I said naïvely, "I understand Miami is very nice." "Miami?" they said scornfully. "We are invited to stay in Palm Beach."

When the lend-lease negotiations moved to the Soviet Union, to become part of the overall trade negotiations, our euphoria mounted. We were going to do something to wind down the Cold War. "City of Peter!" proclaimed Secretary Peterson, addressing a luncheon in Leningrad—formerly St. Petersburg. "Window on the West! Let the winds of free trade blow through . . ." There was music as the luncheon drew to a close. I took my luncheon partner and dreamily we waltzed around, as everyone smiled approvingly.

For all my personal euphoria, some thinking on the American side went too far, I thought. "The Soviets," the commercial officer at Embassy Moscow briefed us, "are conscious that, technologically, they are on a plateau below our own. If we can help them to raise themselves to our level, then we can deal as equals." I remember wondering if we wanted this dangerous country to be all that equal. Some technology transfer, but not too much, I thought, would be about right.

The only really jarring note was Commerce's efforts to dominate the negotiations. Well before the Moscow phase began, their representatives, including a protocol officer, had been in Moscow dealing with their Soviet counterparts, but under strict instruction not to let our Embassy know that they were in town. Surely, we asked, protocol was something we Foreign Service officers were supposed to know about. Not to worry, the Commerce people assured us. Their man had served with the United States Air Force in Germany, where he had dealt with foreigners. Not long after our arrival in Moscow, our Embassy received a telephone call from the

Soviet Foreign Ministry. Someone believed to be a member of the American delegation had been arrested for removing his shirt in front of Lenin's Tomb, during the ceremonial swearing-in of new officers into the Armed Forces of the Soviet Union. It was the Commerce protocol officer, nervously exhausted by the unfamiliar environment and work load imposed on him. To cap things off, Secretary Peterson asked that a member of the State rather than of the Commerce delegation escort the unfortunate protocol officer home. Needless to say, his request was not favorably received.

Tensions between the two agencies never really eased. At one point, I recall Mr. Alkhimov trying to calm down an angry outburst by a U.S. Under Secretary of Commerce against a U.S. Assistant Secretary of State ("Gentlemen, gentlemen, please . . .").

Ultimately, a debt settlement advantageous to both the United States and the Soviet Union was signed. "Thank you, Mike," said Mr. Alkhimov. "I really mean that. Thank you for all you've done." But then, to our dismay, Congress undercut the agreement. The Jackson–Vanik Amendment, an adroit piece of political single-issue activism, made most-favored-nation status further contingent upon the Soviets' release of Jews and dissidents desiring to emigrate. My anger over that breach of diplomatic faith remains undiminished to this day, notwithstanding my own subsequent captivity and my heightened sympathy for victims of human-rights abuse. The motives of the amendment's sponsors had nothing to do with improving Soviet–American relations. And the declared advantage of the amendment to Soviet Jewry was, on balance, negative, since it only infuriated the Soviets, and emigration in fact diminished. Through the confidence that detente would build, our government could probably have done more. As Marshall D. Schulman, a leading Soviet specialist, pointed out in an article in *Harper's* in April 1984:

None of us can remain unmoved by the cruelty with which the Soviet police apparatus deals with dissidents or with those who wish to emigrate. But we should have learned from our recent experience that it is counterproductive for our government to make the human rights issue an instrument in a political offensive against the Soviet Union, and to engage the prestige of the Soviet leadership by frontal, public ultimatums, as it did with the Jackson–Vanik Amendment . . .

As with expropriation, terrorism, or any number of foreign-policy problems, the Jackson-Vanik Amendment raises questions as to how much the confrontational / sanctions approach really achieves. It also illustrates how within our own government, whether the difference is between the legislative branch and the executive, one department or agency and another, one bureau in a department and another, or between sections of the same embassy, we lack the maturity to understand another point of view, to cooperate and develop consensus. Our difficulty in growing up impairs both our view and our management of foreign affairs.

In the fall of 1974 I began a relaxed academic year of study at the National War College in Washington. In August 1975, since I had had experience with Latin American investment problems, I was sent to Chile as economic counselor, the head of the Embassy Santiago's economic section. Louisa and my two older boys, Mark and Philip, went ahead on a cargo boat. After I had finished my Spanish-language training at the Foreign Service Institute, I followed by plane with the two younger boys, Andrew and Duncan, to join Louisa in Santiago. We found a beautiful house, with a small swimming pool, in the suburb of La Reina.

Two years before, in September 1973, the Chilean military, in a quick surgical coup, had overthrown the Marxian government of President Salvador Allende. Their long-expected action was in response to a resolution by the Chilean Senate calling for a military takeover, as well as a decision by the Chilean Supreme Court pronouncing several of Allende's acts unconstitutional. Given the chaos into which Allende's economic mismanagement had thrown the country, the takeover was widely popular. However, the many who expected that the Chilean military would do their constitutional duty, as in the past, and then, calling for new elections, return to their barracks were to be sadly disappointed. Convinced that Allende's coming to power was the inevitable result of the democratic process itself, and that inflation, which was then about a thousand percent, was the result of his ill-advised economic policy, the military were determined to effect radical political and economic reforms, and to stay in power for an indefinite future.

If those who hoped for a return to the democratic process were in for a disappointment, the military were in for a greater one. By expelling a Marxist government, including its Soviet advisers, and doing for the United States in Latin America what, as they reminded us, we had not been able to accomplish in Southeast Asia, the new government hoped to earn American gratitude and economic support. Moreover, in order to solidify that expected support, they had either returned expropriated American investments, such as Dow Chemical, or, in the case of the telephone company and the copper mines, negotiated compensation agreements. What they did not reckon on was the adverse effect of some of their other measures on American, and indeed world, opinion.

The principal concern of the military at the time of the coup was to snuff out any opposition—the displaced regime, they feared, might rally and lead the country into civil war. Thus, they imprisoned, tortured, and often secretly executed Allende supporters. Moreover, foreseeing the high rate of unemployment that their new anti-inflationary program would bring about, along with the possibility of popular unrest, they kept repressive security measures in effect. Particularly in view of Chile's past commitment to the democratic process, American and world public opinion turned against Chile, dashing the hopes of Chile's military for American economic and other support.

In April and May of 1975, as a part of a National War College tour, I had visited Santiago. At that time, American public opinion was just beginning to shift against the Chilean regime. I had accepted the assignment as economic counselor with every expectation of a full plate of responsibilities— Export-Import Bank credits, new private investment, and many others. That certainly was the Embassy's feeling. "You will have all the action," the political counselor, Charles Stout, told me, a bit dolefully. "There simply are no more politics." By the time I returned to take up my duties in August, the American revulsion against Chile was gaining momentum, and the programs I had looked forward to handling were drying up. By contrast, the Embassy's political section was immersed in reporting violations of human rights. "With all due respect to Mr. Kennedy's efforts," I heard Ambassador David Popper point out to a visitor, "this is a political post." My reaction to his comment, I must confess, was not unmixed with concern for my dwindling turf. But my reaction was not entirely self-serving. Why, I asked myself, should an overseas post necessarily be "political" any more than "economic"? However immediately compelling, priorities as determined by Washington should not become the sole filter through which Chilean reality was perceived. Yet the immediacy of Washington's priorities often leave room for little else.

The Embassy's political section increasingly saw Chile largely in terms of human-rights abuses. Its principal contacts were with the opposition Christian Democrats, and some of our political officers became identified with the opposition in the minds of many of Pinochet's supporters. This had the effect of augmenting that section's bias. For my part, I was making something of the same mistake. Although I cultivated relations with certain Christian Democrat economists, and the best economist among my officers, Jim Cheatham, had excellent connections among a wide spectrum of the opposition, my responsibilities tended to take me in the direction of the practitioners of Chicago School economics, today called Reaganomics, who were either part of the Pinochet regime or supporters of it. In time, my views began to reflect those of the people I saw the most. In short, if in Athens I had become part of a "country localitis," in Chile I was part of one "constituency localitis."

In the Embassy itself, then, there were two very different perceptions of Chile, a gap widened by rivalry and infighting between the political and economic sections. Rivalry was heightened by the Deputy Chief of Mission, who was supposed to coordinate all Embassy activities, including the reporting, but whose professional background was entirely political. An Embassy's political function—its political reporting, demarches to the host government on political questions, etc.—was, he told me, "obviously more important" than its economic function. This, I told myself, had to be because it was carried out by political officers. I also wondered what an American politician, to whom it is axiomatic that Americans vote their pocketbooks, with jobs and prosperity coming ahead of everything else, would have made of that tedious discussion. In the real world, politics and economics are interrelated. Neither is "more important" than the other.

In an effort to close the perceptual and reporting gap, Charles Stout, the political counselor, and I went to see Ambassador Popper. He did not see that there was a problem. "I take what I get from the political section and what I get from the economic section and I put them together." He was only restating the classic theory of the civil service, propounded first by Confucius: narrower and narrower responsibilities and outlook as you go down the ladder; broader and broader as you go up. Possessed of the best mind I have ever worked for, Popper was more than capable of putting it all together. What he did not see so clearly were the distortions built into the materials he was getting. Stout and I merely pointed out that integration should begin further down, and left it at that. When I was sent back to Washington on consultation, the desk officer remonstrated with me. "You guys in Santiago have got to get your act together. From the reports we get from the political section and from the economic section, you'd think this was two completely different countries."

More dangerous than all distortions is the Foreign Service view of the world. In this view, Chile, or any country, is a pie. Out of that pie, the Foreign Service slices a wedge and calls it "political," and another, which it calls "economic." There might be other factors of conceivable interest to the United States, but since they are overseen by other agencies, they either turn up in other wedges (agricultural, military, cultural, etc.) or else they simply do not exist. In theory, all the different perceptions are brought together in periodic overall assessments, but in my experience, a truly whole view is rarely in evidence. Partial views of reality are not unusual and are not limited to the Foreign Service. Doctors tend to specialize, and with the same consequences. Like the baffled desk officer who said no one in Santiago was really looking at Chile, so, similarly, one hears complaints that there are not enough doctors willing to look at the overall health of the patient. Academicians reduce knowledge to discrete subjects, specialized to the point where members of the same faculty sometimes find it difficult to communicate. The chargé of one of the smaller embassies in Santiago, where everyone did a bit of everything, mentioned to me how difficult it was for him to communicate with many of his American diplomatic colleagues. Well informed in their narrow specialties, they lacked, he said, the capacity to take an overall view of the country.

In a world in which there is so much potential knowledge to be absorbed, reducing knowledge to manageable categories is inevitable, and not dangerous so long as no one pretends that any particular wedge is anything but a convenience and by definition partial. Unfortunately, the personality that tends to be attracted to a highly structured career like the Foreign Service tends to perceive reality as a series of wedges, and not as a whole. And if nothing of any importance happens outside the segment of the pie that is the sum of all bureaucratic wedges, then the Foreign Service perception will not be all that wrong. But suppose something does happen. In what wedge, for example, would the Foreign Service have placed the ferment of ideas that burst forth in the United States in the 1960s, which was manifested in a variety of ways, such as the breakdown of traditional sexual mores, but which affected the economy and all other aspects of American life? A few perceptive Foreign Service officers, a few ambassadors, might have grasped and analyzed such changes. But not many. Not enough. Certainly the system would not have provided for it.

By the mid-1970s, another shift—a reaction, among other things, to a liberation from traditional restraints, and advocating a return to them—was sweeping the Middle East. The Foreign Service did not anticipate it and did not understand it when it began. Shortly after my return from Iran in 1981, a senior officer in the Department was quoted as wondering how all "that"—the overthrow of the Shah and the takeover of the Embassy—could have happened because of religion. There is no wedge of the pie for religion. Therefore, it lacked significance for United States foreign policy. The Foreign Service sees the world as consisting of sovereign states, each with a government, each government comprised of readily identifiable functions with which embassies can interact. Nothing in its long experience prepared the Foreign Service for a trans-national religious movement of the kind led by the Ayatollah Khomeini. Until its system learns to harness the abundant talent that it has, so as to understand better the world around it, the Foreign Service will continue to be locked into preconceptions that ignore emerging new realities. The Reagan Administration's efforts, in the spring of 1986, to pin the transnational phenomenon of terrorism so largely on one country, Libya, and its ruler, Colonel Muammar Qaddafi, bespeaks the same error.

Religion began to be very significant for me after my first years in Chile. Although I would not admit it even to myself, I was beginning to suffer from burn-out. Bored and frustrated, I chafed at career restraints that had not bothered me before. Strains began to surface in my family relationships, with Louisa, and also with Mark, my oldest son, on his visits from Princeton. In some unhappiness, I spoke to Ray Smith, the Anglican minister of the Santiago Community Church, went through confirmation instruction, and was confirmed by the Anglican Bishop of Santiago, Colin Bazley, who today is Primate of South America. I literally trembled as I took communion for the first time. Full of the enthusiasm that marks a new convert, I agreed to go on a Roman Catholic retreat, which was to be run by charismatics. I had no idea what charismatics were.

On the first day, we broke up into small groups, to be taught to heal the sick. The group leader, Blanca Ossa, turned to me. "All right, so you're faced with a seriously ill person. What do you *do*?" This was not exactly what I had come for, and I had no ready answer. *"Entregarme a la voluntad de Dios,"* I finally replied: Deliver myself up to the will of God. The next day, the schedule called for casting out devils and other evil spirits, which a Jesuit father assured us did indeed exist. So there we were, casting out devils, and during the coffee break a fellow American who had flown down from San Francisco expressly to receive this instruction came up to me and asked, "Have you actually *seen* the devil?" Always the model diplomat, I replied carefully, "Perhaps not directly." "Well," he replied, "I actually saw him sitting on my window ledge. So I took a broom and I beat him."

For a newly minted Anglican, this, plus the glossolalia, where those "speaking in tongues" suddenly take off in a guttural that sounds rather like Arabic, plus the requirement that you throw your arms, in enthusiastic embrace, around people you don't even know, was a bit much. To add to my misery, it was winter, and the seminary was unheated. Along with other "Anglicanos," I used to escape during the guitar playing up to someone's room where a bottle of Haig and Haig was kept available for thermostatic purposes. At that point, my newly found commitment might have ended abruptly but for some words Bishop Bazley said to me at my confirmation. "All right, we've done this for you," he began. Obviously, he sensed a mid-life crisis. "What are you going to do for us?" I volunteered to work in the church's outreach program, delivering food and clothing to the destitute in the *poblaciones*, the shantytowns of the urban proletariat surrounding Santiago like a belt. At every stage in my professional life, I had seen poverty—at a distance. Now I was encountering it face to face. The Pinochet regime's economic recovery program's first priority, the reduction of inflation, was succeeding all too well. Government expenditures were cut in half, and unemployment, officially twenty percent, must have been higher.

As head of the Embassy's economic section, I was approving telegrams analyzing and praising the government's anti-inflationary program. Working for the church on weekends, I would minister to the program's victims. The stench of poverty can be overpowering, yet some shacks were extraordinarily neat. I learned from Ana Muñoz, the block leader in one *población*, that the level of civilization does not depend on the level of one's income. One day she said she would introduce me to a family that was doing well. *"Los niños piden bien"*—the children beg well. I entered the house to see two little faces—I had chased these children from the gate of my luxurious villa two days before.

Yet none of this was giving me what I was looking for. I remember asking myself as I trudged through alley after alley: Just who do you think you're kidding? Your marriage is not in good shape. Neither are you. Things aren't going well at the Embassy. First you've got to pull yourself together before you can be of any help to anyone else. But I didn't know what to do. I was jumping frenetically from one good cause to another, in the hope of finding solace and cure for life's pain. I could not see where the problem lay, which was within myself. I was suffering a kind of moral schizophrenia. What I did at the office, including my endorsement of the government's austerity program, was split off from what I did at church. It wasn't until I left the Foreign Service that I began to pull the two together, to try to reconcile faith with foreign affairs.

As I look back on my days in Chile, particularly toward the end of my tour, I can see where my reconciliation of faith with responsible action might have been accelerated. That is the purpose of Opus Dei, the Catholic laymen's society of which some of my Chilean friends turned out to be members. "We wish we had known," one of them said to me, "that you were a believer!" He particularly approved of the subject for my farewell sermon at the Santiago Community Church, which was the story of Nicodemus. Nicodemus was the law-

yer, the Pharisee and man of the establishment, who pru-
dently made his first visit to Jesus by night, and later became
a follower. After the Crucifixion, when Peter and the other
disciples, lacking staying power and any tradition of leadership and responsibility, ran away, Nicodemus and Joseph of
Arimathea stood fast and did what had to be done. God, I
concluded, needs people like these for his work in the world
as well.

My assignment in Santiago came to an end in the summer
of 1978. Things were getting better at home. But my enthusiasm and my performance were not quite what had brought
me the success I had become accustomed to in previous jobs.
My assignment, back to Beirut as political counselor, was at
a level a bit below where I and others thought I would be by
then. Yet, in some ways, Beirut was a logical choice. I already
knew everybody, from the President of the Republic, Elias
Sarkis, on down. My proven ability to make and develop
contacts, it was assumed, would more than make up for my
lack of experience as a political officer. Part of the arrange-
ment involved several months of an Arabic refresher course
at the Foreign Service Institute, which brought me to the
point, shortly after I arrived in Beirut, where I could manage
luncheons with Shiite notables, and otherwise function well.

Children could not accompany their parents to Beirut. My
two older boys were at college, or beyond. Andrew was at
Groton. Duncan was still too young for boarding school.
Louisa would therefore have to spend the winter of 1978–79
in Washington, until Duncan was ready to go off to boarding
school in the fall of 1979. Then she would join me.

Shortly before Christmas of 1978, I arrived in Beirut for
what turned out to be a disaster. Richard Parker, the Ambassador who had accepted my appointment, had been transferred, and his successor, John Gunther Dean, had his own
view of a political counselor's role, which was to be the Am-

bassador's clerk and rewrite man. Dean did not need my contacts, as he planned to develop his own. My feeling that a reporting officer is as good as the time he spends away from the Embassy, among his contacts, was just wrong for this Ambassador. Dean had an executive assistant who filled his expectations perfectly, and so there was nothing for me to do at this Embassy. By then thoroughly demoralized, I was happy to accept his offer, in March 1979, to terminate the assignment by mutual consent. Before leaving Beirut, I had a long talk with the senior financial officer of the Phalange, the principal Christian militia. "If you really want to stay, Mike, we can easily arrange it through the Israeli Embassy in Washington." Apparently my standing with the Israelis was high. But I could imagine the reaction to that kind of interference, and my chances of getting any assignment thereafter.

When I came back to Washington, I found that assignment doors were closing against me. "Everybody knows that Beirut wasn't your fault," a colleague said. "But, well, you know how it is." Louisa and I decided to dig in and weather it out. We invoked the diplomatic clause in our tenants' lease in order to reclaim our house in northwest Washington, and later, in August 1979, we went off to Maine.

4 / GOING TO TEHRAN

LOUISA AND I were staying with my parents in Northeast Harbor, Maine, when a telephone call came from the Department of State. It was from Henry Precht, Country Director for Iran. I knew before I returned his call that I was going to be offered a position at an Embassy where not many wanted to serve. After the Shah's departure in January 1979, the revolution had peaked with a one-day occupation of the Embassy on February 14. The large American business community was evacuated, and the size of the Embassy and the scope of its activities were reduced. By June, the revolution seemed clearly there to stay, and since order seemed to be emerging out of semi-anarchy, the decision was taken to reestablish the American presence and restaff the Embassy. In August, when I received Precht's call, one position was still unfilled—the financial-reporting job, the same spot in the economic section that I had held in Beirut ten years before. The economic counselor, the head of the section, was in place in Tehran. But since families were not yet permitted to accompany their spouses to this post, he would soon have to come home for family visitation leave. Precht was looking for an experienced officer who could take over in his absence.

The assignment had definite advantages. I had considerable experience in gathering information from Middle East bankers and businessmen. Reporting on an Islamic revolution, given my long-standing interests, would be fascinating. It was a dangerous post, but the situation seemed to be improving. Precht did not mention to me, in the course of that or any other conversation, that he had already alerted Embassy Tehran to the likelihood of the Shah's being admitted to the United States. That would have been a factor in my decision to accept such an assignment. I told Precht that I would consider a temporary assignment of three months, which was finally set at September 19 to December 20, long enough for me to learn something about the Iranian revolution. It was the minimum period for the efficiency report that I needed in order to get my career back in gear, and it would have me back with my family for Christmas. The previous Christmas, which I'd spent in Beirut, had been a lonely one.

Given my later decision to leave the Foreign Service, I have been asked why I was anxious to restore my career momentum. Basically, I still thought of myself as a Foreign Service officer; I needed a job, and I was too proud to give up. My feelings about continuing in the Foreign Service were increasingly ambivalent, however. My fiftieth birthday, when I could retire with a generous annuity, was little more than a year away. I was not exactly sure what I might do if I took early retirement, but I felt I had abilities in me that the Foreign Service had not begun to tap. Louisa put her finger on it: "Don't let the Foreign Service determine your view of yourself," she said to me as I was discussing my future. Although Louisa would have her real-estate business to occupy her, she was far from pleased at the prospect of another separation.

But she was aware that if I was going to stay in the Foreign Service, Tehran would be my last chance. It could also be a new beginning. As a colleague in Washington said shortly before my departure for Tehran: "When you get back, they'll owe you."

Louisa and I came down from Maine early in September and I began to put the garden back in shape. Then I went to the Department to be interviewed by Bruce Laingen, who was back on consultation from Tehran. Since there had been no Ambassador in Tehran since the departure of William Sullivan that spring, Laingen, as chargé d'affaires, was head of the Embassy. When Laingen returned to Tehran, he found that the economic counselor, whose name is unimportant but whom we will call Arthur, had heard of me and welcomed my assignment. At last, I thought, I had a job.

Before leaving for Tehran, I had extensive conversations with "the desk." I spoke with men at the Iranian Country Directorate and particularly with Mark Johnson, its economic officer, who had just returned from a temporary stint in Tehran. He warned me that I would be dealing with the Provisional Revolutionary Government, which, although it looked like and went through all the motions of government, was only a façade. Power resided elsewhere, with the revolutionary and religious authorities. Unfortunately, Johnson's sensible analysis was not always understood at high levels in the Department.

I also talked to Henry Precht. He had just received a telegram from Tehran drafted by Arthur. "Now this," he told me, waving the telegram, "is a *helpful* message." His clear intimation was: "Go and do thou likewise." It was not until I got to Tehran that I became aware of the contents of the message and the problems it was to cause.

On the night of September 19, I landed at Mehrabad Airport. Lonely, and fighting back a sinking feeling over the unknowns I would face in the morning, I also wondered whether this assignment was worth another absence from my family. The next morning, I crossed from my hotel to the Embassy compound. On the compound wall facing the street, revolutionaries had affixed posters denouncing the United States. I had little idea of the size of the compound. The first main building was the brick Chancery, or office building, which looked like a high school. Beyond it, on the right, was the Residence, normally of the Ambassador, now of the chargé. I was soon to reside in both these buildings, in circumstances not of my choosing. Off to the left was the consulate, with its long lines of Iranians as anxious to get to the United States as the revolutionaries were to denounce it.

I reported to the chargé, Bruce Laingen, who got right down to my key problem. Arthur, the economic counselor, was, according to Laingen, extremely sensitive about his position and highly ambitious to succeed in his assignment. Arthur did not quite realize, said Laingen, that not that much was expected of him. I inferred from this, and later confirmed it by observation, that Arthur was trying to do more than provide the information and analysis that Laingen and Washington required. He was trying to define the emerging American relationship with Iran in his terms—with which, as I soon found out, his Embassy colleagues did not always agree. Laingen told me that I was to shore up Arthur's position, and to be very careful of my personal relations. I had volunteered for a job that was below my demonstrated abilities, he went on; that showed, did it not, that I had the capacity not to take unimportant things too seriously. Knowing that it would be a month before Arthur went on leave, I took Laingen's advice very seriously indeed.

I then reported to Arthur, a man younger than I and of rather Prussian demeanor. I had not been with him more than a few minutes before I saw what Laingen had been getting at. I began by telling Arthur of my round of appointments set up by the Iranian desk two days before in New York, with firms whose Iranian assets had been expropriated or whose contracts had been canceled. Mindful of my extensive experience with investment disputes, the desk had thought it would strengthen the section's effectiveness in Tehran. "The desk shouldn't have wasted your time," Arthur cut in. "I do all that sort of thing." Instead, he expected of me the kind of mathematically oriented analytical reporting which, in previous assignments, I had delegated to subordinates. With his graduate-school training in economics, Arthur had earned plaudits from Treasury for that kind of reporting in his previous assignment in Northern Europe. In his haste to achieve ongoing success, however, he ignored certain important differences between Northern Europe and revolutionary Iran.

I tried to explain that I had checked out with the Department the need for sophisticated analysis and had been assured that what official Washington wanted was a better idea of how ordinary Iranians were responding to the revolution. The kind of anecdotal *Wall Street Journal* reporting in which I had made my reputation would be ideal. I could not tell him that the desk had scoffed at the idea of "economic matrices." In the revolutionary circumstances, the necessary data would be unavailable, obsolete, or wrong and would lead to misleading conclusions. My heart sank. Not only was Arthur consigning me to the closet, to do useless economic analysis for which I had little aptitude, but I realized that I would be working for someone who was projecting onto Iran experiences and prejudices that had little to do with the country or its revolution.

There was worse to come. Arthur was at loggerheads with the political section, the cause being the telegram that had reached Henry Precht in Washington just before my departure and that he found so helpful. It expressed a conclusion with which I discovered the political section was in profound disagreement. While the message was still in draft and going through the clearance process, the political section had objected. The disagreement had been brought to the chargé's attention and a compromise hammered out to everyone's apparent satisfaction. Arthur, I was told, went back to his office, revised the message in accordance with his understanding of the compromise, and sent it off, without clearing it once more with the political section. When the political section received their "come-back" copies, the message, according to what they told me, did not correspond with what had been agreed to. In fact, one of the political officers, who by the time I arrived was still smoldering with indignation, was considering sending a message to the Department dissenting from Arthur's telegram.

Arthur had argued that the political climate in Iran was highly propitious for renewed American investment and, by implication, for a reestablished American presence generally. Earlier that summer, when he had first arrived, his initial contacts had been the local agents of American firms, who had sought him out. It was obviously in their interest to convince him, and through him the United States government, that American investors would be welcomed back. Arthur had other sources, he said, who told him the same thing. I made it my first priority to check this out.

One of my early interviews, for example, was with the custodian of the nationalized insurance firms. He was of an older generation, at home in European culture, and spoke excellent English. The high point of his life was during the Mossadegh revolution of the early fifties when Iran had dared to nationalize its oil wealth; prior to Mossadegh, the British government had received more revenue from the oil assets than Iran did. The failure of the revolution, although he was too polite to mention it directly, had much to do with the United States.

Not only had the Central Intelligence Agency helped to restore the Shah, but American oil firms gained a position in Iran they had not held before. It was, he said, placing his hand on his chest, like a pinprick in his heart, never ceasing to hurt.

When I talked about the right of these American companies to compensation, he bridled. But when I put the matter in terms of the desire of the new Iran for fresh technology, capital, employment, and the rest, he relaxed. Of course, he agreed, American firms would be taking a hard look at the promptness, adequacy, and effectiveness of compensation paid by the Iranian government, before risking their own capital in a revolutionary environment. But this gentleman was Westernized. Like Prime Minister Bazargan and the other liberals from the Mossadegh era, he would prove dispensable to the violent religious forces that would soon condemn his kind of liberalism.

Another source on whom Arthur and I together tested out his thesis was Abolhassan Bani-Sadr. The author of the standard text *Islamic Economics*, he was one of the theoreticians of the revolution. After the takeover of the Embassy and the fall of the Bazargan government, he became Foreign Minister and later President. In those roles, he stood out favorably in contrast to the extremists. Because he seemed prepared to be helpful in resolving the hostage question, Bani-Sadr, like Nabih Berri, the Lebanese Shiite leader in the TWA hostage crisis, was characterized by the media and the United States government as a "moderate." In October 1979, however, in contrast to the Bazargan liberals, Bani-Sadr stood out as an extremist. Arthur and I thought he was a real nut.

We arrived at night at Bani-Sadr's house and were carefully frisked, then after removing our shoes at the front door were politely received. The conversation was in French. Arthur raised the question of whether or not the revolutionary government would welcome new American investment. "Of course," replied Bani-Sadr, "provided that it will be for the benefit of the Iranian people, and not for the profit of multinational corporations." Arthur and I could hardly look at each other. This self-described economist would not contemplate, at least for the record, the obvious point that any investment, or business transaction, had to benefit both sides. When we got back to the Embassy, Arthur asked me to prepare the reporting telegram. "But," I asked, "what do I put down?" Nothing Mr. Bani-Sadr had said would make any sense to Washington.

That interview did not shake Arthur's conviction that the revolution wanted a renewed American business presence. He had, he told me, interviewed a mullah, a religious leader, who apparently had assured him that the Islamic revolution had nothing against modern technology. From that, Arthur had concluded that the revolution would not object to renewed American investment and presence in Iran. Never having served in the Middle East, or in any other way been exposed to this issue, Arthur could not distinguish between modernization, meaning certain techniques and equipment, and Westernization, that bundle of secular values, seen to be undermining traditional Islamic and Iranian values, that the revolution was determined to expunge.

We Americans tend to project our values as if they should have universal acceptance. For Americans like Arthur, a desire for investment, which would make Iran more like the United States, was a sign of returning sanity; not to want "progress" was "going back to the thirteenth century." The religious revolutionaries, however, saw American investment as infusing Iran with precisely the Western values and practices they were determined to be rid of. Their feelings were much better understood by the political section, experienced officers, all of whom spoke Farsi and most of whom had served previously in Iran—not just Tehran, but in consulates and Peace Corps centers in the hinterland as well. Their contacts were wide. For example, Michael Metrinko, formerly consul in Tabriz, was on good terms with one of the leading clergy families.

I suspected that the reaction of the political section to Arthur's telegram and to Arthur generally was not motivated merely by his views. Newcomers to a post, including Ambassadors, have been known to change the preconceptions they arrive with, as their experience grows. But, as the political officer who took the strongest exception to Arthur's telegram pointed out, Arthur, not unlike other normally ambitious Foreign Service officers, wanted to achieve something distinctive and remarkable on his tour of duty. He intended to be the first to point out that the widely held skeptical and pessimistic view of the future of Iranian–American relations was not necessarily valid. Most important, the political officers were concerned at the way Arthur used his considerable bureaucratic talents to influence and alter the Embassy's overall position.

Quite apart from my professional concern lest Washington be misled, I had a deeply personal one as well. Experience and instinct led me to side with the hardheaded position of the political section. I wondered what this potential conflict of loyalties would do to my relations with Arthur, and to the efficiency report I hoped to earn.

In September and October of 1979, official Washington was still somewhat polarized in its estimate of the Iranian revolution and of the future of our relations with it. One school of thought tended to argue, and not without reason, that since the revolution was deeply hostile to everything we stood for, we had little future in Iran. The other, led by the Country Director, Henry Precht, preferred to assume that conditions would gradually improve. In the final analysis, they argued, also not unreasonably, that, given its geographic position and traditional ties, Iran would need strong relations with the

United States. The present difficulties should be seen, therefore, as a short-term reaction to the Shah's regime and to our
identification with it. We should take the long view and do
everything possible to improve relations. Arthur's reporting
was just what Precht wanted to have and use to reinforce his
views.

As Country Director, Henry Precht had every interest in
maintaining, and if possible expanding, the scope and importance of his responsibilities. But he was bigger than that. He
had been ahead of the pack in Washington in seeing the
bankruptcy of the Shah's regime. Now he tended to fall victim to the correctness of his past analysis, becoming a parti-
san of the revolution whose inevitability he had so accurately
foreseen. The checks and balances built into the Department's
system of policy analysis did not always work in the case of
Iran. The views of the Country Director tended to prevail, I
often suspected, because the basic concern of NEA, the Bureau of Near Eastern and South Asian Affairs, was still the
Arabs and Israel. Since Iran was receiving less attention, the
Iranian Country Directorate had greater latitude. Nor can this
discussion of policy formulation discount the temperament of
the chargé, Bruce Laingen.

I had not known him before. Others have noted, and I agree,
that Laingen is one of those unusually fine people who see the
best in everyone and everything. He is genuinely interested in
the welfare and personal fulfillment of others. I cannot imagine any nicer man to work for. His sunny and attractive personality had much to do with the relatively high morale of
that difficult post. At the same time, he had some of the defects
of his own virtues. A less compassionate chief might have
enforced more agreement among bureaucratic rivals within
the Embassy, or defined matters of disagreement more clearly.
Above all, Laingen, who had served before in Iran as a junior
officer, was genuinely fond of the country and wanted to see

the best in it. As our day of reckoning approached, we and the nation would have been better served by a chief more aware of the darker side of human nature, better prepared to warn Washington of danger, and to enforce security and take other obvious precautions.

Laingen never fully understood why Arthur was so wrong, nor was I about to endanger my careful relations with Arthur by bringing up the problem with Laingen. But well after Arthur had left on his leave, at our last staff meeting on the morning of the takeover, a political officer just back from a field trip produced evidence of economic chaos in the south. "But that's not what Arthur's been telling me," Bruce said to me, a rising note of concern in his voice. How much damage had Arthur's reporting really done? Immediately after we were taken hostage, before our captors cracked down on any conversations, I stood with a young vice consul in the luncheon line. "Where's Arthur?" he asked, with great bitterness. "He should be here." That vice consul was assigning blame to one man which should have been the whole Embassy's, including me. I could not help laughing, one evening in February 1980, three months into our captivity, when Hossein Sheikholeslam visited the basement room in the Chancery where three of us were confined. He picked up immediately on my mention that I had been in temporary charge of the economic section. "What about Arthur?" he asked. Sheikholeslam had read the captured telegrams. "Who is this fellow? He can't be for real."

As a senior official in the Department once reminded me, there is a great distance between the desk of the reporting officer in the field and the Oval Office of the White House. No single officer's field reporting can be decisive. But it can reinforce a view already held in the Department, on which policy-makers draw. Arthur's reporting, which was used by the Country Director to reinforce his presumption of improving conditions, thereby had an indirect impact on our lack of security. After the first and brief takeover of the Embassy in February 1979, the operative presumption had been one of danger. For example, files were not allowed to accumulate, and papers were routinely destroyed at the end of each day. Rick Kupke, a communications clerk who was a roommate in captivity, told me that by June, as the revolution began to settle down, and parallel with the decision to restaff, the files were allowed to build up, and sensitive documents which had been sent out of the country were returned. When the students took over the Embassy in November, they acquired an absolute bonanza of information.

The return of the files, the restaffing, and the behavior of the staff all reflected a resumption of normality. The staffing of the Embassy and the renewal of Embassy activities were intended to signal American optimism about future relations with Iran. That, of course, was how Americans would interpret it. How Iranian revolutionaries might interpret it was a question no one seems to have asked.

Anyone who had served in the Middle East should have guessed. Like many others in the Third World, Iranian revolutionaries were reluctant to admit that their country's problems were of their own doing; they preferred to blame foreigners— in this case, the United States. So it was necessary for them to believe that the Shah had been our puppet and that the Embassy, under the Shah, had been the "secret government of Iran." Accordingly, they saw the increase in the Embassy staff in sinister terms, arguing that we planned to use the Embassy as a base from which to coordinate a counter-revolution to return the Shah to power, as the Central Intelligence Agency had done in 1953. After taking us prisoner, the students asked where the tunnels were through which, they assumed, orders from American Ambassadors had been transmitted over the years to various Iranian ministries.

The one-day takeover of the Embassy in February 1979 should have alerted the Department of State to the true situation. Had the Department recognized the symbolic significance of the takeover for the revolution, those who did not subscribe to Henry Precht's presumption of a return to normalcy might have concluded, among other things, that the United States should maintain only a modest diplomatic representation in Iran, with minimal staff, housed in an inconspicuous building far from the center of revolutionary activity. If no less vulnerable to attack, a new site might at least have had less symbolic value to potential attackers, as well as containing fewer potential hostages. Instead, in line with Precht's urging, the Department reestablished the Embassy as it had been, not only in number of personnel but in the scope of its activities as well. We seemed to be going out of our way to arouse the suspicions of the revolutionary authorities. Articles about the intelligence activities of the defense attaché's office in fact appeared in the local press. The CIA station was built up, but its members were without the kind of cover that would make their activities inconspicuous and did not have the language capabilities or the Middle East experience that would have made them really useful.

The presumption of a return to normalcy also served as a barrier to our seeing ourselves as the Iranian revolutionaries saw us. Sometimes this was manifested in sheer insensitivity. A CIA officer, for example, serving under the cover of the economic section, crossed the street from the Embassy to his apartment carrying a shopping bag out of which poked the top of a champagne bottle. Alcoholic beverages were prohibited in Iran (but not to embassies), and a revolutionary guard reached in and confiscated the bottle, which gave rise to a minor diplomatic crisis. Worst of all, even Laingen's warnings could not disabuse the Carter Administration of its wishful thinking that relations with revolutionary Iran had improved to the point where they could tolerate a certain amount of strain—including the admission of the Shah to the United States.

For me, in those first weeks, these questions were of less moment than my immediate relations with Arthur. During the month when we were going to work together, how was I going to avoid his pressure for "economic matrices" and establish myself and the kind of reporting I was qualified to do? Fortunately, Arthur had postponed until my arrival a trip of about ten days' duration to the oil country in the south. And as soon as he left, I directed the senior local employee, Mohammad, to set up appointments for me all over Tehran. I then took off, returning to my office to send one or on occasion two telegrams a day to Washington. Language was no problem, since bankers and businessmen in Tehran of necessity speak English.

Suddenly, I felt ten years younger. I was doing what I was trained to do. More important, I felt caught up in the euphoria of the revolution, of people not only free of the oppression of the Shah, but after decades of enforced Westernization, free to be Iranians again, and to make all things new. The question was how far the revolution would go to create an Islamic society, however that might be defined, and whether, at least in the economic field, which was my reporting concern, it would retain Western models. A symposium held shortly before my arrival, whose import was summarized in the press and to me personally by its participants, had been a fiery one. Bani-Sadr and his fellow radicals had come under heavy attack. The Deputy Minister of Trade, an economics professor, told me he had said to Bani-Sadr: "Islamic economics are all very well, but let's stick to the economics we know, which we know will work, at least until we can pull the country out of chaos and get it going again."

The "two economics" became a major theme of my reporting. For example, since in theory Islam outlaws the taking of interest, Islamic economics would not allow banks to charge any. How, without charging interest, were Iranian banks to make any money? As my telegram entitled "Zero Interest" informed Washington, banks could still profit through financial participation in the projects being financed. Since the government had taken over the banks, it would have a major role in determining lending policy, and thus guide the economy while still giving scope to private initiative. And the banking sector itself was to be reformed. Banks, mostly commercial in nature, had proliferated all over the country. Qazvin, a small city, had four commercial banks, three more than it really needed. But the technical banks—the agricultural bank, for example—were all in Tehran and had no branches in the provinces, where they were needed. The commercial banks, therefore, were to be consolidated into four or five or eight (depending on the latest propaganda release) and were to be specialized in various ways in order to foster and improve the development of the country. However, my more conservative contacts in the banking world of Tehran pointed out that the various banks had originally been organized on a variety of Western models—British, Dutch, American—including different accounting systems, which could take years to consolidate.

Arthur returned from his trip south to find a pile of my telegrams. He went through them, shuffling them more and more rapidly in obvious disbelief at their quantity. "You've been working," he said, giving me a quick look. As he read them, I could tell that he liked the product. One of his comments, which cut through to the heart of one of my telegrams, would have capped it off beautifully. He had that kind of mind, as well as a wealth of information about the Iranian economy remarkable for someone with less than six months' experience in Tehran. From then on, he began to relax with me. My reporting was sufficiently balanced that he could not object to any part of it. Although we were poles apart in our view of Iran, I was not about to force any issues. Instead, I worked hard on the relationship, being at pains, for example, to sit on his left when being driven with him in an Embassy car. My restlessness with that kind of thing, which had marred my attitude in Chile, was growing, but I carefully hid it. My career still came first.

Before long, without objection from Arthur, I was sitting in on a meeting between representatives of an American firm whose contract had been terminated and the Iranian authorities. It quickly became clear to me that the American firm had not lived up to its contract. With a quick wink during an embarrassed pause in the discussion, the Iranian chairman confirmed my suspicion that the Americans had obtained the contract by bribing officials of the Shah's regime. Afterward, the Iranian chairman proposed that we lunch at a future date. I was prepared to take him up on the invitation. Once again, I was conscious of a problem that is a constant in Foreign Service life, of conflicting duties and loyalties. Was my first loyalty to Arthur (and to my career) or to the need for Washington to know the truth as I increasingly understood it to be? Back in Washington, was my first loyalty to the United States or to the State Department in its battles with Treasury and Commerce? Here, was my first duty to defend the business interests of these fellow Americans? That was important. But these particular businessmen had struck out from the beginning. After all, I was not their lawyer. But I saw it as my first duty to pursue a relationship with this important, and seemingly reasonable, Iranian official, who would have jurisdiction over expropriation and contract cases involving American businessmen whose hands might be a little cleaner. A few days before the Embassy takeover, I was to deal with questions of loyalty and self-preservation in ways of which I remain ashamed.

About three weeks into my assignment, I secured an introduction to Deputy Prime Minister Bani-Assadi, a son-in-law of Prime Minister Bazargan. Our initial conversation involved a topic as old as Iran, that of centralization versus regionalization. As a student visiting Iran in 1950, I had written a short paper on it, and the elements of the problem had not changed. Over the centuries, Iran had gone through periods in which regional and tribal powers acted as a law unto themselves. The founder of the Pahlavi dynasty (father of the recently exiled Shah), Reza Shah, had pulled the country together after the First World War. Centralization had been regarded as a good in itself, even though, given the venal and corrupt bureaucracy, taxes would be paid to Tehran and not much would be redistributed to the provinces.

Now, with the revolution, Mr. Bani-Assadi explained to me, a move back to regional autonomy was almost inevitable. He was therefore going to put into effect the new management theory he had studied in the United States. In place of authoritarian management, in which decisions come down from the top, the theory envisaged management from below, with decisions working their way up through a series of overlapping committees. Committees at the community level would include representatives of the village, the local municipality or township, and the province. On the level above, the committee would include the municipality, the province, and the ministry in Tehran. Above that, a committee would represent the province, the ministry, and the head of government. Each committee, Mr. Bani-Assadi indicated enthusiastically, would consist of three levels, with the result that an idea originating at the village level could reach to the very top. I did not have the heart to point out to him, whom I saw not just as a con-

tact but as a future friend, that a theory still too advanced
for the major American corporations for which it was designed
might not be appropriate for a developing nation just emerging from a revolution against an authoritarian regime under
which political initiative had atrophied. I also found it curious
that a leader of a revolution wishing to expunge Western ideas
and values was planning to accept implicitly the relevance of
the American experience. But this was still the Bazargan regime, a halfway house to the more radical "revolution within
a revolution" which lay ahead.

The Iranian chargé in Washington, in a conversation with
Henry Precht, had mentioned the revolution's Crusade for
Reconstruction, including its projects in the villages to develop
water supplies, schools, new roads, and communal showers
and libraries. Precht asked the Embassy to look into this, and
I volunteered. I went to Bani-Assadi, who sympathized with
my personal as well as my professional desire to see that
Washington had as complete and accurate a picture of the
revolution as possible. He was also very frank. Unlike what
the Iranian Embassy in Washington had been telling Precht,
the Crusade for Reconstruction was not a result of revolutionary ardor as much as a means to rekindle it. There was concern on the part of the leaders of the revolution, he said—I
had begun to sense it in the crowds—that people were losing
their enthusiasm, that they were hoping for order and calm
after months of turmoil.

Mr. Bani-Assadi was very pleased with the dedication of the
volunteers. The Crusade's projects around Tehran, he feared,
would involve me with students who, he said, were simply too
anti-American. But in Shiraz, things would be different. He
knew the group leader well and immediately arranged my
visit. Larger than I remembered it from 1950, Shiraz, however,
proved to be just as beautiful. The primitive roads to remote
villages were much the same. The projects of the Crusade re-

flected a reaction to the grandiose projects of the Shah, which had been designed to bring prestige to the government rather than benefit to the people. In one of the village projects I visited, a water tower, the designers had dispensed with even the float valve that in every American toilet automatically cuts off the water when it reaches a certain level. If the float failed to work, my student guides told me, it would necessitate repairs the villagers might not be capable of. Stationing a man at the tower to pull a rope to admit water, and, by releasing the rope, to cut it off, was far more manageable.

I admired the student volunteers, with their dedication and their good-humored understanding of the reluctance of the villagers to pay their share of the cost. One student volunteer, a graduate of the University of Louisville, was the son of a local landowner. "I know all these villagers," he told me. "I know how much they contribute. I know how rich some of them are, how poor, and they know they cannot bluff me."

My guides took advantage of a particularly bumpy stretch of road, barely a track, on which several villages depended for access, to remind me that Iran under the Shah had been buying Phantom jets and Tang-class submarines and installing a direct-dial system in major cities for placing international calls. The contrast was stark between rural poverty and underdevelopment and the "modernization" undertaken by the Shah. I could see why these volunteers placed all blame on the United States. We were his model, and he was our man in the Middle East; that was to be the burden of my discussions with my captors as well. Indeed, the Crusade was a parallel organization to the one that took over the Embassy. Some of our guards used to spend part of their free time on Crusade projects, and when we were scattered all over Iran following the unsuccessful helicopter rescue attempt in April 1980, I was housed at least once in a regional center of the Crusade. During this trip to the south, at the date-growing oasis of Jahrum, I was given lunch in a center in which two of my colleagues were later confined.

Back in Tehran, I sent a long reporting telegram to Washington that aroused considerable interest. The desk called, however, to ask the meaning of the phrase "Supererogatory Act of Grace"—words that did not usually appear in Foreign Service telegrams. I explained the term referred to the Muslim charitable foundations active in the villages, which were, in short, doing more than one was really required to. The political section, too, liked the picture I was presenting to Washington of rural life under the revolution.

As I resumed my contacts in the financial community, I began to see increasing evidence of what had been troubling Bani-Assadi: the revolution's loss of verve, the loss of confidence in the regime's ability to manage the economy or even to last much longer. The volatile political climate, I reported to Washington, was reflected in the words of a banker who told me he would do no favors for the revolution lest he end up on its "good" list and then face execution when the counter-revolution occurred. A senior official of the Central Bank was particularly angry at the religiosity which seemed to infect Iranian life. "Do you realize," he asked me, "that I might lose my job because I don't pray?" Others were equally outspoken. One banker said to me, "For God's sake, don't put any mention of my name in your report, because one of these days the students are going to take over that Embassy of yours and they will find the files and then I'll be in real trouble." His name was not known in Washington, but his title and responsibilities carried weight and authenticated what he told me. I cited them all—it is still on my conscience.

The economy itself was not in good shape. It had come to a standstill in February. Then, given the normal desire of people for goods and services, it recovered spectacularly until August. At that point, there came a breathing spell. The merchant class wanted to know what the new constitution then being drafted would contain. How much would it reflect the woolly socialism of Bani-Sadr? And they wanted to know how much longer the revolutionary regime would last. Many gave it only a few months. Factories were operating at fifty percent of capacity; unemployment was disguised because management was forced to keep unneeded employees. The ability of managers appointed for their revolutionary zeal was, in many cases, deplorable. The construction industry, which traditionally had absorbed excess farm labor, was at a complete standstill. Spare parts were in short supply, with importers unable to make the credit arrangements necessary to get them out of customs. As a consequence, banks were highly liquid, interested in rebuilding their deposit bases, but only for short-term lending. Working capital was available, but no investment was going on. Iran had a cash society. Merchants were not only staying liquid but investing in commodities such as saffron, which, with its very high value-to-weight ratio, is handy if you have to leave in a hurry.

All this I reported to Washington. In my last conversation with the desk, four days before the takeover, the economic officer, Mark Johnson, reminded me of the polarization of opinion between optimists and pessimists among Washington's Iran watchers. "Your stuff goes right down the middle," he said. It was as if he were foreseeing my role, following my release and retirement, in trying to explain the realism of foreign affairs to the peace movement, and the peace movement to the Foreign Service. Johnson went on to pay me the compliment that every reporting officer wants to hear: "For that reason, it's being read all over town."

In captivity, during the early days, when we thought we were about to be executed, I had occasion to remember Johnson's words. If Tehran was to be my last job, I thought, I had done it right. Later, I came to realize that it was not good enough. I had reported growing loss of enthusiasm for the revolution, and efforts to revive it. I had not, any more than anyone else in the Embassy, identified what that discontent portended for the United States and especially for its diplomatic establishment in Tehran. As I should have realized, a revolution is at its most dangerous not when it begins but at the moment when waning enthusiasm demands a spectacular and catalytic event, one that will distract popular attention from mounting problems and justify the further radicalization of the revolution. The United States government, by admitting the Shah, provided the excuse for such an event, which made possible the "revolution within a revolution."

Of course, none of these factors could have been apparent to the Department, or to the Embassy, in the early days of my assignment. There were student demonstrations near the Embassy compound, to be sure, but their clamor, often as not, had to do with such university problems as student housing, not with perceived iniquities of the United States. Living was easy. Bruce Laingen's great gift being his concern for his staff, provision was made, and rules sometimes bent, to make life agreeable. I swam nearly every morning in the chargé's pool, decorated my apartment with relatively inexpensive Baluchi tribal rugs, began to entertain and to go out socially. For a small fee, Embassy cars with drivers could be rented for excursions into the countryside. Arthur and I spent a day driving to Demavend, through beautiful valleys east of Tehran. I finally felt that I was getting through to a personality not unlike the Foreign Service itself, with a narrow perception of the world but, withal, likable. And he, clearly, felt less threatened by me.

In mid-October, Arthur went home on family visitation leave. At that point, some important personnel decisions were being made. The Provisional Government did not want an American Ambassador. Laingen, who had hoped to be named, was therefore looking for another assignment. Although nominally chargé d'affaires, he was actually Deputy Chief of Mission—the key man in every Embassy, who, under the Ambassador's direction, coordinates everyone else's efforts. Because Laingen was trying to do both jobs, coordination and follow-through at the Embassy, especially on chores such as the reduction of files, was poor. The lack of a DCM was to be most keenly felt during the takeover, when Laingen was at the Foreign Ministry.

With Laingen's departure a growing likelihood, the need for a DCM became even more critical. Arthur surprised me by proposing my name and by canvassing on my behalf. I was under no illusion about some of his motives. In his battles with the political section, his position could only be strengthened by having in the catbird seat an economic officer indebted to him. But I will not easily forget his words: "I will serve you as loyally as you've served me."

When he reached Washington, Arthur began to sell the desk, and Louisa, on the desirability of my assignment as DCM. Wives, the desk pointed out to Louisa, were soon to be allowed to join their husbands. Louisa was not taken with the prospect. Her Washington real-estate business was going well. And her instincts, refined by years in the Middle East, were telling her to stay away from Iran. But I, looking back on my standing of only a few months before, felt that I had come a long way. Whatever might happen with Arthur's proposal, my Tehran assignment would carry me forward again in some way.

When did I first begin to suspect that things were seriously turning against the Americans? In my first round of banking interviews, a very senior banker had refused to see me, sending word that he could not afford to see anyone from the American Embassy. Many others, as we have noted, were willing. Another indicator, much later on, was a leak to the press by the Minister of the Interior of an official conversation with our chargé. Under instructions from Washington, Laingen had questioned why the revolutionary authorities had to execute some elderly senators from the Shah's regime, men reportedly in their eighties. The local press seized upon his demarche. The headlines screamed: "America protests the shooting of CIA agents." Iranian unwillingness to agree to an exchange of Ambassadors was another portent of trouble.

When Arthur went on leave and I took over his duties, my level of concern was fairly low. But when on October 22 Bruce Laingen, his face showing worry, told me that the Shah had just been admitted to the United States, not only I but the whole Embassy, down to the lowest-ranking member, knew we were in for trouble. I was not to know, until the students circulated it among the hostages, that Laingen had received a letter from Precht, the Country Director, advising him as early as August that pressures in Washington to admit the Shah were building but that no decision would be made without consultation with the Embassy and a review of its security arrangements. There were no consultations. Laingen was notified of a decision already taken, and instructed to seek and accept the Provisional Government's assurance that we would be protected. I remembered Mark Johnson's warning, before I left for Tehran, that the Provisional Government was a mere façade. On Sunday, November 4, we saw the Provisional Government's assigned guards shaking hands with the students pouring in to take us hostage.

Back in Washington, Louisa learned through her real-estate connections that the Shah, from his Mexican exile, was negotiating to buy a house near Purchase, New York. Treatment of the Shah's cancer was not the only reason for his move to the United States. He intended to take up residence. When in an angry moment after the Embassy takeover, Louisa threw this in the face of the Under Secretary for Political Affairs,

David Newsom, he looked stunned. Later that evening, Newsom called Louisa to ask if she was feeling any better. Foreign Service wives are not expected to question official wisdom.

For some time before the Shah's move to New York, Henry Precht had been scheduled to pay a routine visit to us in Tehran. As it happened, his departure was set for the day the Shah arrived in New York. When he reached Tehran, Precht said nothing, at least not to me, about the reaction in the Department to the Shah's arrival and what it meant for us. Much later, after my release from captivity, I had coffee with Precht in the Department cafeteria and he told me that just before his departure for the airport he had been called by his immediate superior, who urged him, "Don't go out there, you'll be *killed.*" "But," the former Country Director continued, "I felt that my place was with all of you." I expressed my appreciation for his courage; I could not help wondering to myself about the Department's level of concern for the safety of the rest of us. I asked Precht why he had said nothing to us, and Precht replied, "When I got out there, you all seemed like such good soldiers that I stopped worrying." Precht not only stopped worrying; he positively exuded optimism. One morning, in the main drawing room of the Residence, he addressed what was left of the American business community in Tehran. "Recently," he said, "I gave a speech to a group of congressional wives. Afterwards, one of them came up to me and asked: 'Aren't you very brave to go out to Tehran?' Now, I ask you, isn't that silly? Who in their right mind would imagine that Americans in Iran are in any danger? Yet that is just the attitude that we in Washington have to put up with."

Why didn't I, why didn't the others at Embassy Tehran, tell Precht what nonsense this was? Why had we not alerted Washington to the mounting danger? Several months later, in our basement room, Hossein Sheikholeslam was to raise the same issue. "Every street child in south Tehran knew that we were going to knock over your Embassy. Why didn't *you?*" Embassy personnel in those last two weeks lived in a kind of dream; we experienced varying degrees of apprehension which we found ways to deny. The Halloween Ball at the Residence was beautiful. Small groups chatted easily on the verandas. Bruce Laingen, as always, had put his friendly stamp on the evening. I even taught my secretary, Kathy Gross, how to waltz.

Reinforcing that denial of danger was part of our dedication as professionals. We had volunteered to help restore Iranian–American relations. We could not admit to ourselves the extent to which our mission had been fatally undermined by President Carter's decision on the Shah. Precht's observation that we were "good soldiers" was indeed accurate. It remains the answer to another of Hossein Sheikholeslam's puzzled questions: "But if you knew you were in danger, why didn't you just leave?" No one did. After all, we were members of the Foreign Service, or of the Armed Forces, of the United States. We were also Americans, and our perception of foreign reality, including the dangers facing us, was distorted. Because so many of us at the Embassy liked Iran, and viewed revolutionary aspiration for it with considerable sympathy, we found it hard to grasp the depth of the revolutionaries' hatred for what we represented. We did not imagine the power of religion as a political force, especially when it deepens hatred. For all my own experience in the Middle East, my learning process really began with captivity.

Although our mission was now an impossible one, the Department continued to build up the Embassy staff. A new commercial officer, Robert Blucker, arrived. To introduce him, I arranged a party on October 30. He had come, as I had, via New York, where he had made the usual rounds of major banks and corporations with interests in Iran. At the

Chase Manhattan Bank, he told me, he was ushered in to see David Rockefeller, whose role in securing the admission of the Shah was soon to become public knowledge. "Well," Rockefeller told him, "you're going out to face the music." At my party, I repeated Blucker's account to the representative of the Chase Manhattan Bank, who regularly visited Tehran. "Oh," he said, laughing, "David always worries. I've told New York that there's nothing to worry about."

Another addition to the staff was a CIA officer assigned, for cover purposes, to the economic section, with a cover-job title of economic / commercial officer. Somewhat concerned, I went to the CIA station chief, to discuss what this newcomer's specific duties would be. Most of the economic staff, I pointed out, were locally recruited Iranian citizens of long tenure and experience, who would be quick to spot anyone without a credible economic or commercial portfolio. Moreover, we had to assume that our local staff was under pressure to report to the revolutionary authorities. This difficulty had not occurred to the station chief. What did I have in mind? The Embassy, I pointed out, had no labor officer. That, he replied, was an ideal cover, giving the new man the excuse he would need to get out of the Embassy compound and become involved in his covert activities.

Before the officer's arrival, I directed Mohammad, my senior local employee, to arrange an appointment for the new man with the Deputy Minister of Labor. Thus, the man was "working his cover" even before he got off the plane. I planned to introduce our new labor officer, along with the new commercial officer, to my Iranian contacts at my cocktail party. Everyone accepted the invitation, I thought, for reasons which owed less to my social charm than to Islamic prohibition. Embassy parties had become convenient water holes for the faithful. Unfortunately, neither the station chief nor I had taken the precaution of clearing the new man's designation with Victor

Tomseth, the political counselor, who, when he found out, objected violently. He demanded a review by the "country team," the Embassy's section heads. His underlying problem, the station chief and I agreed, was with Arthur, the economic counselor, who would soon return to his post. From Tomseth's point of view, it was hardly desirable for Arthur to be given another reporting channel, that of the Department of Labor, by which to promulgate his views. And so, on Tuesday, October 30, the morning of the day our new labor officer was to be introduced at my party, the Embassy's senior officers, including the chargé, met to decide whether or not to strip the CIA officer of his cover.

We met in the tank, the Embassy's secure area, which had the additional advantage of sealing off the ugly sound of hostile demonstrations in the street outside. I was silent while Tomseth made a fine and in bureaucratic terms virtually unanswerable presentation. Labor, he noted, was a political function. Labor officers competed for promotion in the political cone. Moreover, the new man did not speak Farsi. How could he deal effectively with labor-union officials who spoke nothing else? I thought, as he went on, that if I based my argument on the danger a CIA officer would face if his cover were blown, I would sound like an alarmist and lose. "This officer," I conceded, "does not speak Farsi. He would indeed require an interpreter. "But," I added, speaking slowly for greater effect, and with my pulse beating faster, for I was engaged in the kind of bureaucratic dueling which I still loved, "he does speak the language of labor. He has worked on a factory floor where he was a shop steward." As was his custom, Laingen reserved judgment, but Tomseth suggested lunch. His manner indicated a willingness to deal. So the cover held until the takeover, when the chargé's safe, containing the names of all the Embassy's CIA officers and their cover jobs, fell into the hands of the students.

On the morning of Wednesday, October 31, I called on Deputy Prime Minister Bani-Assadi. My purpose was to thank him for having arranged my trip to the south, and to report my impressions of the Crusade. Mr. Bani-Assadi was troubled. Why, he burst out, would the United States government not grant his government's request that Iranian doctors in the United States, known to the Provisional Government, be allowed to examine the Shah? We both knew that no one in Iran had swallowed the medical pretext for the Shah's admission to the United States. Revolutionary elements constantly invoked the role played by the Central Intelligence Agency in restoring the Shah to power in 1953. A medical report would at least weaken the force of their argument that the United States was about to do so once again. I replied that I thought a medical report would be forthcoming.

A massive demonstration against the Embassy, Bani-Assadi went on, was scheduled for the next day, Thursday, November 1, a religious holiday. Finally, he observed that students in the Crusade for Reconstruction were getting out of hand and refused to cooperate with officials of the Provisional Government. I already knew that students in Tehran and Isfahan had been taking over hotels, in order, they said, to obtain adequate lodgings.

Bani-Assadi was trying to signal something important and urgent. I returned to the Embassy to report the conversation to Bruce Laingen. Much concerned, he told me that he had received a message that the Shah's family had vetoed any idea of a medical examination. At Laingen's direction, I reported my conversation with Bani-Assadi by telegram to Washington.

Back in my office, I found the head of the United States Chamber of Commerce, an old Tehran hand who had an Iranian wife. We talked about the students and their hotels. "If," I asked him, "they are taking over hotels and the government can do nothing about it, what will they take over next?" The thought that we might be next had not really sunk in. This was denial at its most straightforward. Had the British government, for example, been the object of mounting revolutionary suspicion and hatred, then I might have foreseen that its Embassy would soon become a target. Reasoning backward, I might have concluded that the students, whose patience with the moderate Provisional Government was running thin, were testing limits, to see how far they could rock and discredit the regime. Reasoning forward again, I could even have foreseen that by taking over our Embassy, as they had done in February 1979, they would once again force the Provisional Government to back the United States against the revolutionaries. This time, with the Shah in the United States, and given memories of the American role in restoring him in 1953, the regime would be placed in an even more impossible situation. But it was we, not the British or anyone else, who were involved. I could not think objectively in the face of repressed fears for my own safety, and my hope, equally unacknowledged, that there would still be an Embassy over which I might be DCM. At the same time, I was beginning to feel distinctly uneasy.

My Chamber of Commerce contact left, and I went over to the Residence for an informal luncheon in honor of a Foreign Ministry official. Exuding his usual optimism, Laingen pointed out that he had great confidence in Iran and the future of our relations. Excusing myself, I went back to my office to keep an appointment with Leigh W. Hoagland and Norman Fashek, two visitors from the London office of the Bankers Trust in New York. They were well informed and asked searching questions. Khomeini, I assured them, had matters well under control. No one should be alarmed. This, I thought, was what Laingen would want me to say. But I can still sense the queasy feeling in my stomach as I said it. This was the only time that I, an economic-commercial officer who had always tried to play it straight with the American business community abroad, ever misrepresented what I really thought to be true. Later, after my release, I sent an apology to Hoagland. He sent back word that he had not believed me. Still later, Hoagland told me that upon his return to London, on November 2, he was ready to sound the alarm.

Later that afternoon, I had my usual Wednesday telephone conversation with the desk, and with Louisa, who had come into the Department for my call. Sure that the Embassy would be attacked, she begged me to take some leave, to go to London, for example, for my birthday on November 5. What could I say? She was right. If I admitted it, she would have been even more upset and, knowing Louisa, all the more determined to get me out. I wanted to tell Mark Johnson straight out just how dangerous I was beginning to think our situation was. Instead, not quite able to say it, I used subterfuge. I knew that Arthur was scheduled to address a group of business executives in New York the next day, so I said to Johnson, "For God's sake, don't let Arthur get out on a limb. Things are getting worse out here."

After our release, I found that a member of our political section had been contemplating a dissent message to the Department, warning of the dangers we were in. But he never sent it. Afterward, the Department was to explain that it had never received from the Embassy a clear, clarion note of alarm. I certainly sent no dissent message. A few years back, when my career prospects were very promising, I might have taken the risk. But the memory of being jobless was too recent for me to take any chances now.

At the end of the day, on Wednesday, I went to see our security officer, Al Golacinski, to ask him what our chances of survival were. "If anything happens, Mike," he said, "we're on our own." I went out to dinner that night with an Iranian couple, with whom I behaved rather strangely, making inappropriate remarks, as if my social fine-tuning was off. What, I asked myself, when I got back to my apartment, is the matter with you? For the first time in my life, I was beginning to have intimations of my own mortality.

The next morning, Thursday, November 1, from my apartment overlooking one end of the Embassy compound, I could hear the noise of the demonstration at the other end. How can we run an Embassy under circumstances like these, I asked myself. Inside the Chancery, Rick Kupke watched on closed-circuit TV as a demonstrator reached the top of the compound wall. Why aren't we being evacuated, he thought to himself. He transmitted Laingen's reporting telegram, which just presented facts, without recommendations. After the demonstration, as I walked around the compound, a Marine commented to me, "Man, we're going to have a real Alamo!"

Friday and Saturday, our regular Muslim weekend, were quiet. My feelings of tension eased somewhat. I played some volleyball and drafted a long telegram in response to one received from the Department. This was not the time, I argued, for the United States government to insure new American investment in Iran.

Sunday, November 4, began a normal Iranian workweek. Entering my office, I found a pink slip, a notice of a security violation. For the second time that week, the Marines had found my office safe left open. Security violations had never been a real problem. What really was happening to me? With ominous thoughts of a full-scale security reprimand, just what I didn't need, I went to the staff meeting. That morning it was held early because the chargé and the political counselor had an appointment at the Foreign Ministry. They left and I returned to my office. Then a Marine came running down the hall . . .

5 / HELD HOSTAGE

AS THE SECOND morning of my captivity broke, I tried to take stock of my situation. In the house outside Tehran to which the students had moved us, we were no longer blindfolded, but our hands were tied. I was sharing a bed with two naval officers, one of whom I will call George and the other Sam. I knew neither of them, and each had particular problems. Sam had to be the world's worse snorer. George had been among those who, following the surrender of the Chancery, had held out in the communications vault in order to shred the central files. When the vault was finally surrendered, he was badly beaten. Still in a daze, he was unable to control his diarrhea, or to perceive the importance to the rest of us of cleaning up its effects. After about a week he slowly returned to normal, at which point Sam reminded him that some laundry had to be done, and he did it.

The double bed was in the corner of a small, third-story bedroom. Through the window—though we were expressly forbidden to look out of it—I saw a large swimming pool, a wall, a road, some other houses, and hills in the distance. On foggy but not on clear days, we could hear the drone of aircraft. This meant, according to Sam, who was a naval aviator, that we were under the instrument-landing path of a major airport, probably Mehrabad. For a hostage, any such piece of information, however trivial, seems important. The well-appointed modern bathroom down the corridor confirmed that this was the suburban house of someone with Western tastes. A single patent-leather lady's shoe from Paris, left behind in one of the closets, surely suggested a hurried departure. Later in our captivity, we were to find ourselves housed in other confiscated residences throughout Iran.

Blindfolded every time we were led to the bathroom, we exploited our other senses to find out all we could about our surroundings. The sound of voices, together with that of weapons being broken down, told us where the students' ready room and arsenal were. They had a radio, and once I thought I could hear English spoken with a Georgia accent, presumably President Carter. From the way voices seemed to carry from the floors below, and from fleeting impressions gathered in spite of blindfolds, we surmised that the house had a large center well; the ground floor was the living room, and our corridor seemed to be a balcony overlooking the living room. We could sense the presence of, and occasionally hear the voices of, Embassy colleagues in neighboring rooms. One of them, presumably to let the rest of us know where he was, "hit the deck" with a crash that was followed by the sound of student guards running from their arsenal. Most but not all the time, a student sat in our room. His absence was the occasion for whispered conversation, "dona speak" being the injunction most commonly repeated by the students.

Students and hostages alike played the orientation game. On occasion, as we were being led down the corridor, our guards would spin us around in order to disorient us. They laughed as they caught us counting our steps to the bathroom. After less than a week in our first bedroom, we were moved to another room, in which the bed was ten feet away from the window, to make it harder to peek out. As before, three of us had to share a double bed.

Peeking, to orient ourselves and to make some contact with the outside world, was to be a pastime throughout our captivity. In each new place, I peeked once, if at all. In these early days, I watched Sam, with a roguish expression on his face, waiting until the guard stepped out and then scampering over to the window for his peek. In other ways, as the three of us, terrified, sorted out our roles and responses, our differences said as much about our backgrounds, whether military or Foreign Service, as about our individual personalities. For example, the guards, once we reached the bathroom, allowed us our privacy. One day in our first week, without asking permission, I took a shower. Like the guards, who quickly moved to impose a limit of two showers per man per week, my military roommates were very surprised at my presumption. It was, after all, unauthorized.

I soon learned, after being led back from the bathroom, to retie the cloth binding my hands myself, since that way they were invariably more loosely bound than those of my roommates. "How very State Department," snickered George. What I considered ingenious was, for these naval officers, only demeaning. Moreover, they were horrified at the way I argued back when students tried to indoctrinate us with films about America's "great crimes against Iran." "Shut up, Mike," Sam whispered, and then, to the students, brightly, "Go on, we're here to learn." That kind of acquiescence I considered demeaning. Also, I was already worried about being put on trial and about the record our responses might be building up.

These minor cultural differences notwithstanding, we agreed on fundamentals. "Look," Sam whispered, "we're all going to have our ups and downs. Let's help each other whenever we can." From the first day, Sam and I called for soap, tooth-

brushes, an electric razor, and towels. We did our laundry
no matter how bleak things looked or how depressed we were.
At our insistence, the students brought us fresh underwear,
pajamas, and a community bathrobe. And one day a beaming
guard brought me a red armchair. From sitting on the floor,
and from nervous tension, I had developed lower-back pain.
I realized that our captors had a gentler side, which had only
to be taken advantage of, and with that in mind, I learned
to treat them as stewards in a private club, with the kind of
courtesy that produces that extra degree of service. Every
time they did something for me, I thanked them. A later set
of roommates followed this policy, to the point where one of
the guards said, "My English is not all that good, but you
three seem to be . . . gentlemen."

From the only instruction we Foreign Service people had
had before going overseas, a one-day anti-terrorism seminar
at the Foreign Service Institute, I knew that we should try to
make the students aware of our own humanity. Tell your
captors, the training film had made clear, about your wives
and children, show them photographs if you have them, and
find interests in common, such as playing chess. In the beginning, I made the mistake of asking the students their names.
To them, this suggested counter-intelligence work. Yet it was
clear, from the way a particularly harsh guard quickly disappeared, not to be seen again, that our captors wanted good
hostage-guard relations. Later, as we were moved all over the
country, I saw the same screening process at work.

Before long, all the guards with whom we had any contact
were English-speaking. They seemed to be uncertain about
the purpose of holding us. One objective, apparently, was to
send us home prepared, if not to defend their cause, at least
to evidence some understanding of it. Hence, the distribution
of pamphlets by the Islamic modernist theologian Ali Shariati,
the propaganda films, and the discussion periods. For that

propaganda to be in any way successful, however, they should have given us some assurance that we would in fact be sent home. But within our first ten days of captivity it was made clear to us, albeit indirectly, what might happen if their demands were not met. "When," Sam asked a senior guard, "will we be going home?"

"We hope so," replied the guard, adding quickly, "We want the Shah." My roommates thought this implied an intention to send us home. I had no illusions. I lay in bed, wondering when my government's refusal to return the Shah would exhaust their patience and we would have to die. Like many other Foreign Service officers, I had for a long time espoused the hard line associated with Dr. Kissinger. A Foreign Service officer had to expect that he might be taken hostage and that he might be held for ransom. The United States government should pay no ransom at all, that doctrine went, lest a precedent be established that would endanger Americans around the world. "All right," I could hear myself saying, "we might at the beginning lose one or two Foreign Service officers." Now, as one of them, it behooved me to rethink that position.

I tried to convince myself that, after all, there was a major difference between paying ransom and the extradition to his own country of a national against whom a case of murder, extortion, and a variety of other crimes could readily be made. And did we not, I asked myself, have a right to consider our relations with revolutionary Iran? Returning its archenemy, the Shah, might go far to clean the slate of grievances that the revolutionaries held against us. I was still thinking, of course, in terms of the mission that we had been sent out to accomplish. Each time I thought of a new and more convincing argument, however, a wave of despair overtook me. It was like trying to pretend that a loved one recently dead has not died, or that a love affair unhappily broken off is still on. Reality, when it reemerges, is all the harder to take. Reality,

I knew, meant that, whether or not the Shah should be returned to Iran, the United States could never return him while we were held hostage.

What I could not know in those early weeks was that the Shah was only the ostensible reason for holding us hostage. The other reasons, as some of the students were to concede and as we have already noted, were to bring about the revolution within a revolution, to replace the moderate Bazargan government with more radical elements, and to keep revolutionary fervor at a high pitch while new institutions were being set in place. But, unlike the TWA hostages, who in 1985 gave press conferences and could listen to the BBC, we had no news at all. As a senior guard explained, "If we give you news, you will have ups and downs. Better"—and he made a kind of horizontal smoothing gesture with his hands —"that we tell you nothing at all." And we could not guess that as soon as Iran's revolutionary institutions were in place, in September 1980, Khomeini would propose conditions for negotiations that eventually resulted in our release. These terms had nothing to do with the original demand for the return of the Shah, who had died the previous July.

This brings us to the question of whether or not we should negotiate with terrorists. During the TWA crisis of June 1985, Henry Kissinger appeared again and again on television, preaching a doctrine not merely of "no ransom" but of "no negotiations." In January 1983, I had discussed the issue with him, mentioning my musings in captivity, including the fact that "we might lose a few Foreign Service officers." Kissinger interrupted, "But you don't have to lose any. That's the point." He evidently still believed that if the United States government only stands firm and denies terrorists an opportunity to present their demands, then there will be no reason to take hostages in the first place. No hostages taken means no execution of hostages.

I wondered, as I listened to him, what might have happened if the minority view among our captors had prevailed and we had been led to the execution wall. But Kissinger's theory has conceptual flaws deeper than what this one contingency might suggest. What Middle East terrorists demand at the beginning of negotiations and what all along they are really after and what they are willing to settle for are usually three quite different things. The Kissinger thesis confuses the three. Let us begin with the difference between what they say they want —their up-front demands—and what they really want. Denying terrorists the opportunity to make their up-front demands will not deter their taking hostages if the motivation is other than the up-front or stated demand.

Middle East terrorists have pursued a range of objectives inspired by varying levels of psychological, political, and cultural factors. In the case of the Iran takeover, our captors' declared objective, the return of the Shah, was separate from their real objectives, which included the revival of revolutionary ardor, the political radicalization of the revolution, and the establishment of revolutionary institutions. In the hijacking of TWA 847, rivalries among Shiite groups made each group seek an objective different from the declared objective of liberating their co-religionists held in Israel. In all Middle East terrorist undertakings, the need to publicize the cause supplies a major but certainly not the only objective.

Underlying and reconciling all these objectives for the terrorist is what, to use old-fashioned anarchist language, we may call "the Deed," a semi-mystical, almost ritualistic, often self-sacrificial concept of the act. Through it, devotees consecrate themselves to their cause.

In the case of Muslims, whose faith ensures to martyrs access to a more blessed hereafter, that motive is especially strong. In the case of Palestinians, "the Deed" is an assertion, through risk and self-sacrifice, of the national identity, the existence of which the principal target countries, the United States and Israel, have denied. "The Deed" serves to bond, to pull adherents together and attract support from others. It also gives expression to psychological and cultural needs. For Palestinians, Israel is not merely the usurper of their homeland but the symbol of the culturally dominant West. One reaction reinforces the other.

A refusal to negotiate addresses only the up-front demand, not their underlying motives and objectives. Since the up-front demand is usually the less significant motive, it is difficult to see how the Kissinger thesis can deter terrorist acts. Neither is it particularly useful in resolving hostage crises once they arise. Not only does Kissinger fail to distinguish between the up-front demands and more basic objectives; he also confuses all these objectives with the alternatives that the terrorists might settle for. The task of the negotiator, assuming the up-front demands are unacceptable, is to discern which alternatives might be consistent enough with the terrorists' real objectives, and to persuade them to accept those.

A refusal to negotiate only holds the terrorist to his up-front demands, which may be unacceptable. Negotiation affords time for both sides to consider alternatives which each can accept without loss of face. Moreover, since terrorists in preparation for a takeover have become "psyched up" and capable of violence, it is all the more important to begin to negotiate as quickly as possible. Patience may save lives.

Unlike the TWA hostages, who individually or through their representatives were exposed to the media and world concern, we were told by our student captors that we had been abandoned, that "Carter is doing nothing for you." Trying to think of something encouraging, I whispered to my two roommates that we civilians had two labor unions, which might remind those in charge that there were hostages in

Iran. To myself, I fantasized a protest parade of relatives up Pennsylvania Avenue, led by my wife and four stalwart sons. Sam suggested that we had better develop all the rapport we could with our guards, since we might have to negotiate our way out on our own.

Through all this, the fear of death, like a specter, was in the next room, ready to pounce. One evening, I heard someone addressing a meeting at the bottom of the stairwell. He finished, there was a pause, then someone else closed the meeting with "Allahu Akbar," the rallying cry of the revolution. The tone was "All right, let's do it." A student returned to his station in our room, his face set. What, I asked myself, fighting down a clammy feeling, had they just been told? How much time was left to us, before the students lost patience with Washington's refusal to deliver up the Shah? One morning, not long after that meeting, the students without any explanation blindfolded us, marched us out into the corridor, and gave us the usual disorienting spin-around. Then they took us to what we could sense was a smaller room and sat us on the bed. We waited, with a growing certainty that we were in a holding room, that we were about to be led out and executed. The acrid smell of fear was overpowering. Still without explanation, we were told to get up and were led to still another room. Our blindfolds were removed, and with a great sense of relief we recognized our own room. Three students were disconnecting the vacuum cleaner, having completed an overdue cleanup of our quarters.

On about our third day in the suburban house, the students distributed Bibles. I grabbed one, and in due course found the passage in II Timothy where St. Paul says: "Remember that Jesus Christ of the seed of David was raised from the dead according to my gospel. For which I am imprisoned as a common criminal, even to the point of chains, but the word of God is not chained." I recalled the sermon preached in Boston not long after World War II by Pastor Niemoeller, an anti-Nazi leader, which we heard about at Groton. Every day, in the concentration camp in which the pastor spent the war, he would repeat to himself this great testimonial, and it had strengthened his faith and his morale. Now I, a prisoner far from home and in fear for my life, my hands tied as a symbol of bondage, thanked God for my Christian faith.

We lived in constant fear of being executed, in those early days, and concentration and reading were difficult. But in time I began to read more. Since I love plays, I had reached for an anthology in the first distribution of books. The first play in the book was *Danton*, in which at the end of Act III the hero is led out into a tumbril that is to take him to the guillotine. The next play was *Mary Queen of Scots*, which ends with her death on the chopping block. I then turned to a book by Admiral Richard E. Byrd, called *Alone*. In it, the explorer describes wintering over in the South Pole by himself. Often, he was faced with a difficult choice. If he turned off his heater, he would freeze to death. But if he left it on, a gas leak could suffocate him. Byrd comments that, as you live with the prospect of death, nature has a way of making you numb to it. I passed the book on to Sam, and the next day he motioned to me (the guard in the room did not allow us to speak to each other) and pointed to the same passage that had struck me.

One midnight about three weeks into our captivity, as I was trying to sleep, some students came into our room and removed my red chair. Then I saw my clothes being taken from the closet. Convinced, as was Sam, that my time had come, I lay there, throat dry, knees twitching, until dawn. Then, since nothing had happened, I struggled out of bed and asked to be taken to the bathroom. On the way, I looked into the closet. My roommate's clothes had also been removed. Someone had decided to force us to wear pajamas, the usual

Middle East prison garb. I resolved not to be caught psychologically unprepared for death again.

On another occasion, also at midnight and about five weeks after the seizure of the Embassy, the senior guard entered our room. "All right," he said quietly, "let's go!" He returned the clothes in which we were taken captive. When asked whether we should take our toothbrushes, he answered, "Leave them." Pajamas? "Leave them." Books? "Leave them." For the first time, they replaced the cloth strips which bound our wrists, and handcuffed us. They then covered our heads with blankets and loaded us into a van, which drove off into the night. I prepared for death. I reviewed my life, asked forgiveness of my Creator for things I had done or left undone and gave thanks for all the blessings I had received. At that moment, looking squarely at myself and at my life's end, I experienced a serenity that I had never felt before.

The van slowed down and stopped at a lighted doorway. We were taken out and led upstairs to a bedroom, where the blankets were removed from our heads and the handcuffs were replaced with cloth strips. There were six hostages, and together with our student guards—the one time this happened—we all bunked down for the night. The next morning, Sam went into the attached bathroom, where he found a glass tumbler with the U.S. ambassadorial seal on it. We were back in the Residence, in the middle of the Embassy compound.

If anything, the feeling of fear was stronger than it had been in our suburban house. When students guarding the perimeter of the compound opened fire with submachine guns, we had no way of knowing whether those were random volleys meant as deterrents to the howling mob outside the compound or an execution squad at work.

The following night, I was moved to yet another room, my shift being the result of a minor drama of which I was unaware. Bob Blucker, the commercial officer, was a fanatic non-smoker. When Rick Kupke, the communications clerk, was moved in with him, Kupke lit a cigarette. "Either he goes," said Blucker to the students, "or I go." And the students were so taken aback that they moved Kupke out. I, a non-smoker, replaced him. There I found our two senior military officers, Colonel Thomas Schaefer, the defense attaché, and Colonel Charles (Chuck) Scott, the head of the military mission. They were keeping count of the volleys. The next night, two students came in and told Tom Schaefer to get dressed. Then came Chuck Scott's turn. He began the familiar litany: Shouldn't he take his towel? and so on and so on. My legs began to twitch. But by the time one of the students came back for me, they had become aware of the anxiety they were causing. "Only moving to another room," he assured me. I wound up back in my original room, where Rick Kupke tried to be reassuring. "If every volley were an execution, we'd all be dead six times over."

I now saw a choice looming up, between waiting to be executed and trying to escape. In our new room, my "bed"— two chairs pushed together—was next to a window that led onto a balcony. Beyond the balcony, there should be an awning extending down to the patio around the pool where I used to swim every morning. Our guard would step out of the room periodically. Suppose I were to slip out the window and down the awning and hide in one of the changing rooms? After the hue-and-cry was over, say the following night, I could run to the compound wall, clamber over it, and on to freedom! Then I returned to reality. Suppose the guard came back while I was climbing through the window? Suppose I slid down the awning into the muzzle of an Uzi held by a trigger-happy perimeter guard? Nearly fifty years old, and unathletic at best, could I ever outrun these students? Suppose I made it to the compound wall. Outside, the mob ceaselessly chanted: "Makbar Amreeka!" Death to America. How would they react to a real live American suddenly materializing at the top of the wall?

But if I had not at least tried to escape, how would I feel when they propped me up against the execution wall? How much of my reluctance to move was simple inertia, how much the weather? It was bitterly cold outside, and my bed was warm. I tossed and turned all night, cursing myself for some kind of Hamlet. Finally, I decided that if they had wanted to shoot us, they would probably have done so already. Time, I told myself, is on the side of the hostage, as his captors develop an increasing investment in him—usually, but not always. The next day, they moved several of us to a room with only mattresses on the floor—a room from which escape was impossible. I felt relieved. By what process, I began to ask myself, do people reach such difficult decisions? It was a subject I was to deal with professionally after my release.

On December 16, a student entered the room. He was smiling ingratiatingly. "Would you like to write a letter?" he asked us. The invitation had never been extended before. One of my roommates whispered, "You see, that's the last thing they get you to do." His explanation was soon reinforced by the aroma of steak—the traditional last meal. I wrote to Louisa:

> All of a sudden we have been told that we can write a letter. Whether this is just part of the considerably improved conditions that recently have been extended to us or whether this is a "last letter" is not entirely clear. If it is the latter, I face it with unexpected serenity . . . I have no bitterness about anyone or anything.
>
> But if it is only the former, then the experience I am going through will serve us both well. Dr. Johnson wrote that the prospect of hanging concentrates the mind wonderfully. In short you tend to pull everything together and try to figure out what is or is not important.

How much one lets little things get in the way, particularly the hazards of a career, social standards—the
whole bit. So much seems to depend on how others rate
you, and there is never enough time to appraise and
reappraise one's self.

One night not long afterward, when lights were out and
the student guard had stepped out of the room, one of my
roommates spoke: "What have I done in my life to deserve
this?" There were sympathetic murmurings from the other
mattresses. I was silent, but in my mind I asked: Do you
really believe that your past conduct has anything to do with
it? You must imagine that, somewhere up there, there is a
celestial judge, and a cosmic prosecutor, and a heavenly public defender! All you have to do is to make your case. Let's
say you've been an efficient and loyal public servant, a loving
husband and father, a devoted son. As soon as the judge hears
this, you'll be exonerated, and won't have to go through the
hostage experience any more.

Why, I thought suddenly, we're all lucky to have been
born. Haven't I sailed out of Northeast Harbor on a northwest
day? Other memories, crowding in, were almost more than I
could handle, and I stopped. But I had never before pondered
my life in such terms. It was as if the props which had been
supporting me—the "right" education, career, and social status
—had been knocked away, leaving me with only the question
whether and how I was going to die.

On another night, the guard having left the room, the voice
of Barry Rosen, another roommate, rang out: "Only five more
shopping days before Christmas." We laughed hysterically.

The students distributed a press release. The Imam Khomeini had announced that "serious priests" could minister to
the hostages at the Christmas season. I wondered what sort
of clergyman would be acceptable to the revolution. A few

days later, we heard an American calling out: "Merry Christmas." From below, a piano began to play "O come all ye faithful." Our hands were untied. I put on my coat and tie. We were blindfolded and led downstairs. "Maybe," I whispered to one of my roommates, "it's some liberal like William Sloane Coffin." Then the students removed our blindfolds. Blinded by the sudden glare of television lights, we entered the main living room of the Embassy. Along the wall sat the students, faces immobile. This was their big moment on TV, but it was also an opportunity to see how the Christians would behave. In the middle of the room was a figure in a red academic robe, smiling warmly. It was William Sloane Coffin.

I had met Bill Coffin two years before, in Chile. A group of relatives of the "disappeared" followers of the late Marxist President Salvador Allende—people unaccounted for following the military takeover—had staged a sit-in. Bill Coffin had come down to bear witness to it. Like the rest of the Embassy staff in Santiago, I was deeply sympathetic to the plight of the relatives. At the same time, I was impatient with the readiness of activists like Coffin to rush into sensitive situations which they could not fully understand and where they might do more harm than good. As if anticipating such a reaction, Coffin in his call at the Embassy in Santiago had been somewhat defensive. When Ambassador George Landau, who had replaced David Popper, remarked that the participants in the sit-in were taking their instructions from the Communists, Coffin turned in his seat, almost ready to pounce. "How do you know?" "Because," returned the Ambassador blandly, "we hear instructions being relayed to them over Radio Moscow."

Now in Tehran I was a prisoner, frightened, for once one of the disadvantaged of the world, and I felt Coffin's welcoming smile and a rush of relief. I greeted him, reminding him that we had met before. Five hostages sat on a sofa and two chairs, and a student sat with us, to be sure that we did not talk to one another. Coffin asked us to choose our favorite carol—it turned out to be "Silent Night"—and sat down at the piano to play it. None of us sang very well. Then he asked us to read aloud in turn from the Scriptures. The Nativity story from Luke—"And there were in the same country shepherds abiding in the field, keeping watch over their flocks by night" —fell to me. I knew it by heart, but it was as if I were reading it for the first time. As I approached the end, I gave it all I had: "Glory to God in the highest, on earth *peace*, good will toward men." I hoped that somehow this message would reach the students around us, whether they spoke English or not.

Coffin then leaned back in his chair and delivered a short sermon. "What a way to celebrate Christmas!" he began, his eyes taking in our surroundings. "But doesn't this make Christmas all the more important?" Short, relevant, sensitive to the lack of religious belief among most of the hostages, his sermon was one of the best I have ever heard. He realized how bitter we must feel, but we must not let bitterness consume us. Instead, like a river that runs deeper when its banks narrow, our confinement should give us the opportunity to go deeper, to reexamine our lives.

Coffin managed a few words alone with me. He had seen Louisa on TV, with Barbara Walters. He relayed a message from my mother, that my wife and boys were "excellent." More generally, he told me—and this came as a complete surprise—the whole country was concerned. "People talk about nothing else." Whether or not we knew it, he went on, he felt that we had been betrayed. It was perhaps too early to educate the American people as to why this had happened, but . . . He had hoped to be able to tell us all that was being done on our behalf, but the students would not let him. In any case, "we" hoped to get "you" out in a few weeks. The implication of his words was that the U.S. government, still in the thrall of the Shah, was not going to do much for us, unless its hand was forced by liberal activists like William Sloane Coffin and a movement which, as he had during Vietnam, he might again spark. "And now," he concluded gently, "you have to go back there." All of us were troubled by the propaganda use to which we knew the students would put this religious service. Rick Kupke, unimpressed by Coffin, wondered, "What's in it for him?" But I was profoundly grateful for Coffin's ministry. And that gratitude persists, though today we are barely on speaking terms.

All through the service, the pile of Christmas cards on a large table distracted me. Were we at long last to receive some mail? It turned out that they were addressed to us as a group. Each of us was allowed to pick up a handful. After we were led back to our room, we sat in a circle on the floor, with a student listening in, and discussed them. This was the first time that some of us had heard each other's voices above a whisper. Our hands were left untied. One card was from a seventh-grade class in Fort Lee, New Jersey. "The Shah is an oppressor who should be extradited, but you cannot hold America hostage." More might be said on the subject, but I doubt that the essentials could have been stated any better. The realization slowly came to us that we had a concerned nation behind us.

The next day, we had Christmas dinner—turkey, cranberry sauce, yams, all the fixings from an Embassy commissary stocked for Thanksgiving before the takeover. In the middle of dinner, the Ayatollah Montazeri, the "chaplain" to the student movement, came in to greet us. His speech, translated by Barry Rosen, was cordial. He realized that we were victims of circumstances; he trusted that the U.S. government would take a more sympathetic view of the problems of the poor, and he hoped that with the aid of Jesus Christ, whose birthday we were celebrating, and the cooperation of the U.S. government, we would soon be free. The cumulative effect of Bill Coffin, the Christmas cards, the dinner, and Montazeri's greetings led us to the heights of optimism. "I'm going home," whispered a roommate, who evidently began to count the days. When release did not occur, he suffered a nervous collapse. Another of my roommates, Larry, began to bombard the bemused guards with written proposals for ways to effect our release. Several of these had him returning to the United States to negotiate our release with the United States government, of which he was an employee! One, at least, of his submissions, parts of which he whispered to us, envisaged the sudden appearance of Jane Fonda, Coffin's associate in the anti-Vietnam campaign, waving a release order. My own skepticism about our prospects did not sit well with him. I had listened harder to Montazeri's "cooperation of the U.S. government" than to his "aid of Jesus Christ." My attitude, Larry whispered, bespoke a death wish on my part.

About midnight one evening between Christmas and New Year's, a volley of shots sounded from outside. Guards came running, taking up positions in the hallway. Terrified, we pressed our faces into our mattress. Only the demeanor of our room guard, who sat impassively in his chair, led me to suspect that it was just a drill. That afternoon, the students had put up a poster on the wall by the door to our room. It showed Carter holding an old-fashioned scale, with two trays. On one tray were the hostages, and on the other the Shah sitting on piles of money; Carter's fingers were weighing down the Shah's tray. At the end of his watch, the room guard made his final rounds, checking each of us. Then, just before he left the room, he ripped the poster off the wall. He was not the only Muslim gentleman I encountered in the course of my captivity.

Just before New Year's, the student we came to know as Mohammad the Mover turned up to move us. When I was finally allowed to take my blanket off my head, I found myself in a cramped, cell-like basement room, obviously a local employee's office in the basement of the Chancery. I had two roommates, Rick Kupke and Larry. Our depression was such that Kupke at first could not make up his mattress. As if in partial compensation for a considerably reduced life-style, and given that we were easier to manage in these smaller rooms, a student assured us, laughing, that he no longer had to tie our hands. We had merely exchanged quarters with our captors. They, realizing as we did not that we were all in for a prolonged siege, had chosen to move to the more comfortable living space of the Embassy Residence. On New Year's Eve, as midnight approached, our guard very conspicuously withdrew in order to let us talk. With tumblers of cold water, we drank in the New Year.

6 / MOCK
EXECUTION,
RESCUE ATTEMPT,
AND RELEASE

ONE EVENING EARLY in February 1980, as Larry, Rick Kupke, and I in our basement room were preparing to settle in for the night, the door burst open to reveal masked students shouting "Savak," as if this was a raid by the Shah's secret police. Despite their masks, I recognized Hassan, the student usually in charge of taking us for showers (by then reduced to one every ten days). This had to be some kind of charade—but we could never be sure.

Blindfolded and led out into the freezing corridor, we were told to undress down to our shorts, and were lined up with our foreheads and hands against the wall. Behind me, I could hear the students chambering their weapons. Other hostages, I learned later, felt the muzzles of submachine guns pushed into the napes of their necks. I was wearing jockey shorts. Students took turns pulling at the elastic waistband and snapping it against my back. I resisted the thought that part of the cause of my trembling might be fear. The beheading of Charles I, in January 1649, also took place on a cold day, and the King insisted on an extra undershirt, lest he tremble from the cold and be thought to be afraid to die. I began to remind myself of everything else I knew about Charles I, until, after an interminable wait, we were ordered to dress. (After my release, as I lecture at schools and colleges, I use this episode to dramatize the value of a liberal education.)

Back in the room, I gave a restrained cheer. Somehow I felt I had passed a test. Kupke smiled, feeling much the same. Larry said nothing, being still very frightened. He had been half asleep when the students burst in, and he could not be so sure it was only a charade. We found our room in disarray, and my belt and razor were missing. Later we learned that there had been a suicide attempt among the hostages; the students had used the precautionary shakedown as an opportunity to terrorize us. The room guard did not return to take up his station. Clearly, they were giving us the chance to discuss what had just happened. We decided to play it their way and admit that we had been frightened, that we knew who was boss. When Hassan came in and sat down at the guard desk, he waited for us to open the conversation. Oh, we had been taken out into the corridor? That must have been the special security force, about fifty students, nobody we knew. We acknowledged that we had been given a lot to think about, which pleased Hassan. I did not let on that I had recognized not only Hassan but several others.

I found it interesting that the students had felt the need to terrorize us but at the same time to deny personal involvement. Later some of the students apologized to some hostages for the episode.

That they had adopted the "Savak" disguise was significant: they were a study in ambivalence. About a week before, when Hassan had dropped by our room for a political discussion, I had taxed him with the ambiguity of his position. "All right, Hassan. You argue, and probably correctly, that the Shah should come back and stand trial. Among other things, he locked up his opponents without letting them know the nature of the charges against them, threatened them with execution, mistreated them, cut them off from contact with their families . . . and allowed them showers once every ten days. And, of course, far worse things. But if these things were bad, what are you doing to us?" Hassan had the grace to look embarrassed. "We are punishing America, not you," he replied, and left the room.

Hassan was at least aware of some moral ambiguity in the taking of hostages. Others among the students, victims to a greater or lesser degree of victimization, were not. "You are being held in order to punish America for its great crimes" against the Iranian people committed either directly or through the "puppet Shah." They, the victims of these crimes, felt morally justified in retaliating and in repeating some of the very offenses committed by Savak.

In January, there had been a kind of sea change in the mood of our guards, the recognition that we were in for the long haul. "Good morning, Mr. Kennedy," said Little Hitler, as we called the most objectionable of the guards, "how are you this morning?" And by mid-February we had been moved out of our cramped quarters in the basement to a comfortable room on the first floor. From its windows we could see high-rise buildings across Taleghani Avenue. From time to time, we had dinner by candlelight. And soon we received permission to speak to one another, and the full-time room guard was withdrawn. By then, too, we had come to know the students. Some told us their real names: Ahmad, the economist, who after the aborted rescue attempt in April 1980 was to become senior warden; Abbas, not one of the original guards, who used to listen to Louisa on the Voice of America ("Your wife," he would tell me, "is doing so much to effect your release"); Ali, known as Little Dwarf because he was so short, who tried to start a consolidated laundry service for the hostages. After two weeks of mismatched socks, we told him we would prefer to do our own. But he continued conscientiously supplying us with vitamin pills.

Others were known to us by their nicknames only. There was Tooth, for example, so named because of a conspicuous gap; his name we learned after our release, was Hossein Sheikholeslam. Psycho, our cook in the latter days of our captivity, was, we thought, well named; he made excellent lasagna. There were Croquet Mallet, Brillo Pad, and the Barber. But the most complex of all was Mailman. He was tall for an Iranian, and his real name was Hamid; on January 3, when he entered our room for the first time, he brought us letters from home.

The students were governed by committees, of which the security committee was clearly the most important. Other students, presumably from different committees, had specialized functions. Tooth dealt with our indoctrination. Whenever we moved, Mohammad the Mover seemed to be in charge. Mailman, who seemed to be the coordinator, told us that he was keeping files on each prisoner. He took a parental interest in his charges. When, for example, we asked about a colleague one of us had seen quite by accident in the washroom and who seemed depressed, Mailman responded, "Yes, he has been depressed, but now he finally understands that he will not be shot. Besides, his wife has just sent him a lovely picture puzzle!"

Whenever a Muslim clergyman came to visit, Mailman, who had discovered that I spoke some Arabic, would get me to say something in that language. As we spoke in Arabic, he would stand by proudly, like a parent basking in a child's accomplishments. He liked to give us things—not only mail, but candies and cookies—and he expected us to be grateful. Not that he was personally at ease with all the hostages. In our room, two of us had advanced degrees. Perhaps we were too well educated, too sophisticated. We knew that he spent a great deal of time with the younger Marines, whom he thought he could dominate more easily. Many Marines, who referred to him as Eel, simply despised him. "Some of the hostages," he said to us, a baffled look on his face, "are very severe."

Occasionally, Mailman's quest for our gratitude overstepped his authority. For example, he told us one day that we could receive food packages. We decided whose family was good for peanut butter, whose for pâté de foie gras, and wrote accordingly. Two weeks later Mailman came back, somewhat shamefaced. "President Carter went on national TV to tell the American people not to send you food packages. We do not understand why he did that." At another point, having forgotten his first explanation, Mailman told us that the students were refusing all food packages addressed to the hostages, on the theory that the CIA would poison the food and blame the students for murdering us.

Mail, being uncertain, was a constant strain. One day I lost my temper, and Mailman was furious. "You will not curse me," he said and stomped from the room. Later I apologized. The next day, Mailman appeared with some color photographs of my parents' home on the Maine coast, taken from a letter I was obviously not going to receive. "I thought," he said, "that these would look nice on your wall."

Mailman thought of himself as an organizer, a talent which found an outlet in getting the hostages a library and other amenities. He was particularly proud of his videotape theater, to which he would convene his charges in the small hours of the morning. We would be led staggering sleepily down the corridor, our faces masked with towels, each with a hand on the shoulder of the person ahead. Mailman's favorite TV serial was *Lucan*, the story of a boy brought up by wolves, later found, and then raised by humans; we soon wished Lucan had remained in his original habitat. Mailman, who was surely a sentimental person, liked the most saccharine Walt Disney films—most objectionable of all, *Fantasy Island*. And however tactfully we tried, we never did manage to turn his attention to some of the more interesting film cassettes piled up on the floor. He saw himself as an authority figure. This was his videotape theater and his decisions were not open to question.

Together with Hassan, Mailman had gone into business. They had appropriated garbage bags from the Embassy commissary and were looking for ways to market them to Iranian housewives. They wanted the three of us to provide them with American-style advertising copy. Rick Kupke and Larry did most of the work. "Housewives," our copy began, "don't litter! Use Baggies!" I doubt that we were any threat to Young and Rubicam, but these two black-marketeers were more than satisfied.

In mid-April, an International Red Cross representative, Harold de Gruerick, came to visit us. Among other things, he expressed concern about the lack of fresh air and outdoor exercise. Mailman responded that he had set up a Ping-Pong room with a bicycle exerciser and barbells. "Have you seen this room?" the Red Cross representative asked me. "No," I said. "The students tell us there is one, but every time we ask to go there, they tell us it is occupied. We are beginning to wonder if it really exists." Afterward, Mailman came to us, very distressed. "Why didn't you tell me that you weren't going to the Ping-Pong room?" Soon we were using it regularly.

There had been another, more serious crosscurrent during that interview, however, and Mailman knew it. De Gruerick, the Red Cross emissary, had told us that a number of hostages had been interrogated extensively about their alleged intelligence activities before the takeover, to the point where some were suffering from depression. Had this happened to any of us? No one replied, because no one dared. As the representative asked his question, Mailman kept his eyes fixed on Rick Kupke. Shortly before, he had detained Kupke in the library and cross-examined him on why he had helped destroy the central files. Unless Kupke "confessed," Mailman warned him, he would be placed in isolation, or worse.

When during the takeover the door to the communications vault was finally opened, hours after the rest of us had surrendered, Kupke had been held to the floor with a knife blade to his eyes, and had been told that he would be blinded if he did not disclose the combinations to the safes. No communicator memorizes the combinations to any but his principal safe. "I don't know," he kept repeating, "I swear I don't." Eventually the students relented, and later individual students expressed regret for this violence.

Mailman knew there was nothing to be learned from Kupke. His interrogation had been an outlet for the cruel streak, curiously combined with gentleness, that characterized many of our guards. "Don't ever forget," Mailman reminded us, "we can keep you tied to chairs for the rest of your time with us, or we can kill you." As the Red Cross representative prepared to leave, I got him alone briefly and in French, which the students did not speak, told him, without any specifics that we were indeed being harassed.

From the beginning of our captivity, the students made an effort, if not to convert us, at least to make us see the merits of their faith and cause. They quite consciously revealed much about themselves, when, for example, they were anxious to establish that the evils of modern Iran, a tyrannical Shah, Savak, a venal bureaucracy, widespread incompetence, poverty, and many other things, were not the fault of the Iranians. Americans, foreigners, were at fault; to the revolutionaries, the Embassy had been the secret government of Iran. Early in our captivity, in the suburban house where we were shown a propaganda film about the shooting down in Jaleh Square, in September 1978, of students by the Imperial Guard, our guard observed: "We cannot believe that it was really Iranian troops that fired on the students. Iranians do not kill other Iranians. There had to be sergeants from the U.S. Military Mission standing behind them, telling them where to shoot." I could not help smiling, and recalled that more than twenty years before, a Palestinian friend had explained why they had lost Palestine to the Israelis. "It was British intelligence that made us Palestinians conspire one against another. They weakened us, and made it easy for the Jews to run all over us."

We all rationalize away our failures and shortcomings by attributing blame to others or to outside circumstances. In the Middle East, or in any area colonized or semi-colonized by the West, such rationalization is endemic. Weak governments, lack of technical progress, and a diminished sense of cultural identity in contrast to the vitality and self-confidence of the West—all these can generate low self-esteem. It has to be compensated for and rationalized by blaming the Westerner for whatever happens. And it is easy to ascribe all evil to the Westerner, since so often the Westerner is the actor and the Middle Easterner the acted-upon. The British did indeed have a policy of divide and rule, in Iran as in Palestine. The Americans not only coordinated the restoration of the Shah in 1953 but boasted about it. The Shah become known as our man in the Middle East. What else could these students consider him but an American "puppet," and us the people responsible for all his misdeeds? Every rationalization contains such a kernel of truth. The students wanted to expand it, to document past misdeeds and fix the blame on the United States. What better sources than the Embassy's archives? Hence, the priority given the central files, and the threats to Kupke. The students went to incredible lengths to collate the shredded documents which fell into their hands.

On the night in December 1979 when we were moved back to the Embassy Residence, we were put into a room that had not yet been cleaned after the students had occupied it for a month. There I came across a draft of an open letter to the American people by then Foreign Minister Bani-Sadr. Although many Embassy documents had been destroyed, what was seized, he said, proved conclusively that the United States government had indeed been the secret government of Iran. Iranian weaknesses could be excused, he was really saying; a balm for their self-loathing was at hand. The foreigner would once again take the blame for everything that had gone wrong. By the same logic, the nationalist, the post-colonial terrorist, finds justification in taking any measures he feels necessary to obtain revenge.

Such rationalization was one part of our student captors' thinking. Another was their mixed feelings about America, a combination of admiration and resentment. They used to tell us: "We have nothing against you personally. We like Americans. It's the United States that we hate." Part of this split in their attitude toward the American people and the U.S. government was based on their perception of history. The U.S. government had supported the Shah, had helped to train Savak, had collaborated with Savak in monitoring dissident students in the United States, and, very important, had "waged war against the helpless people of Vietnam." It was, however, the American *people* who had forced the withdrawal from Indochina. This persuaded our captors that a fissure existed between the government and the American people, one which they hoped the hostage crisis would widen. Later some were disillusioned by the extent to which the hostage crisis had pulled the country together. But this did not diminish their professedly high regard for the American people, if only they could get to them with "the truth."

On a deeper level, the students were coping with highly ambivalent feelings about our country which are difficult for us to understand. They were reacting to our successful and dominant culture, which in fact pervaded every aspect of Iranian life and which was the target of the revolution that these students were the vanguard of. For all its great past, present-day Iranian culture offered little, especially in science and technology but in other fields as well, to compete with the West. Engineering students from one of the world's oldest cultures studied engineering in English. These were students at the cutting edge of a revolution whose goal was to expunge Westernizing influences from Iran, and they were internalizing those very influences. The strain must have been great. Making a distinction between the American people and the government, what is admired and what is the object of hatred, is a classic way of coming to terms with ambivalent feelings. Equally natural is the desire to strike back, to find some way to humiliate a person whom you admire who makes you feel inferior. This can take the form of seizing an Embassy and holding its staff, and indeed a whole nation, hostage.

For these students, there was an on-going American connection which took several forms. I recall one student who dropped in on our basement room sometime in January, to chat with his friend, our room guard. Generally, our guards prided themselves on their green fatigues, the "in" uniform. But this young man was a vision of preppiness—sports jacket, button-down shirt, tie, gray flannels. "Where are *you* going?" I asked him. "I'm returning to Georgetown," he replied. Among the older group, a number of students, including Hossein Sheikholeslam, who had attended the University of California at

Berkeley, had studied in the United States. Others had followed programs in Iran modeled on American curricula.

I am often asked whether this older group, in their late twenties or early thirties, were really students. They had been students in the early 1970s and had helped to found student resistance organizations at the time. They were leaders of these organizations, and when the Shah's regime turned oppressive, they began to despair that they could achieve the Iran they wanted by other than revolutionary means. If the older men among our captors were "leaders of a student organization," the rank and file who guarded us were, for the most part, full-time university students. "You know," one of them complained to me, "my parents are getting after me because my grades have fallen. I'm spending too much time guarding you." To which I made the obvious suggestion.

Few of the students, however—even among those who had studied in the United States and whose English was very good—really understood our country and its political dynamics. In this regard, Hossein Sheikholeslam was perhaps an exception. Commenting on their efforts to generate American support for their cause, he told us, not altogether unreasonably: "We are concentrating on certain academic groups and clergy, and, very slowly, we think we are having some success." As for the other students, the America they described was in many ways unrecognizable. It was a projection of the Iranian experience. They saw a country where a very few rich dominated a seething mass of workers waiting for the opportunity to revolt. They hoped that taking the Embassy— the kick in the pants they were delivering—would promote a worldwide revolution, including a revolution in the United States.

They had apparently never heard of Archie Bunker, and they didn't understand that blue-collar workers are the most nationalistic of Americans. They also had high expectations that American students would protest, as they had at the time of Vietnam, and force the return of the Shah. One day in early January, our guards played us a tape from the United States, featuring "Death to the Shah," a folk singer's protest song. "Get out of Iran," the folk singer demanded. The student who had brought the tape stood by smiling and proud, totally unaware of how unlikely it was that American students would take political action. American students were no longer being drafted to fight an unpopular war, and, like all Americans, they were primarily concerned about getting the hostages home.

Like Americans, whose unquestioned myths about their country color their view of other nations, our captors saw the outside world and the support they might get in terms of their self-image. Whereas our self-image is one of invincibility, they saw Iran as victim and sufferer, a view which Iranian diplomatic history over the last hundred years would do much to sustain. But, fundamentally, their world view was shaped by Shiite myth, notably that of Husain, grandson of the Prophet, who in the seventh century was defeated and who died at the hand of the wicked Caliph Yazid. Behind Husain's martyrdom stood Shaitan, the devil, who works through earthly agents like Yazid. Translating the myth into modern terms, they saw Carter as the Great Satan, and in the cartoons we were shown he was always depicted as the devil. The Shah, Carter's agent or puppet, a latter-day Yazid, had oppressed the Iranian people, who stood, of course, for Husain.

Given a world view that was essentially diabolic and fraught with their own suffering, it was only natural that our captors would seek other sufferers who, they assumed, would make common cause with Iran. For example, in Khomeini's announcement made just before Christmas 1979 that "serious priests" would be permitted to visit the hostages, he appended the hope that some of these would be black, since American blacks, like the Iranians, had suffered at the hands of the United States. And just as Americans are puzzled whenever reality does not conform to their self-image, so too, our captors had difficulty understanding why so many whom they considered fellow sufferers did not rally to the Iranian cause.

The negative reaction of the American black community was a disappointment to them. But one extremist group of Native Americans, the Indian Treaty Council, made common cause with our captors, to the point where some of its adherents, acting out the students' fantasy that the CIA was interfering with our mail, actually carried letters from Iran across the Atlantic to my parents' home. Native Americans enjoyed a place of honor in the students' pantheon of the oppressed. The paperback edition of *Bury My Heart at Wounded Knee* was to be seen sticking out of the pockets of the Marine fatigues the students had taken and wore. Rick Kupke, who is half Kiowa, benefited from this pro-Indian feeling. He received more mail than any of the three of us, and was the first to make the one and only telephone call we were allowed to make to our families.

When the hostage crisis failed to generate the support our captors hoped for in the United States, they blamed the media. "Your media have stirred up nationalism against us," Hossein Sheikholeslam said to us. Their feelings about the media became very mixed, indeed. Having failed during the closing years of the Shah's regime to awaken interest in his human-rights abuses, they now found themselves, as Mailman told us proudly, "on prime time." Such exposure generated high expectations, which in turn brought a double letdown when our media failed to publish their press releases. Mailman, for example, complained that one of Khomeini's most important statements had been ignored. "What did the statement say that was so important?" I asked. "It was the Imam's letter to the Pope at Christmas," he replied. What did the Imam say to the Pope? Apparently he had said, "If Jesus Christ were alive today, he would condemn Jimmy Carter." So the students had to seek an explanation, and it was, clearly, that the media were "disinforming." Somewhere they had picked up that word, along with "controlled." We asked, "Mailman, who controls the media?" "It's perfectly obvious," he said. "They are controlled by David Rockefeller and the Zionists."

In blaming the American media for their inability to get through to the American public, our captors refused to face the extent to which they had bungled their own propaganda: they had failed to sort out their objectives in holding us. Their first attempt was to persuade the hostages to identify with and support their cause, and then they would use us to convince our countrymen. For example, at the outset of our captivity, a number of my colleagues were persuaded to sign a petition calling for the return of the Shah. The inducement, of course, was the suggestion, if not the promise, that those who signed would be released.

For some reason, I was never presented with such a petition, but I resolved to refuse to sign. How well I would have adhered to that resolve under strong pressure, I will never know. Later, in February 1980, when the students demanded that we write to our hometown newspapers in support of the return of the Shah, I responded with a three-page screed to the *Bar Harbor Times*, full of State Department gobbledygook and self-contradictory statements: ". . . that the Shah might be returned in the context of ever-improving U.S.–Iranian relations"—all mush, which I felt confident would never leave Tehran. Similarly, I fudged my responses in an interview with Mary, as Nilofar Ebtaker, the students' TV propagandist, was nicknamed.

To be successful, such propaganda efforts would require that the hostages have some sympathy for their captors' cause.

That would have required that the students, at a minimum, suppress their resentment against the United States, to the point where they accorded us consistently decent treatment. Instead, being neophytes, they could not handle their ambivalent feelings toward us. They allowed themselves on occasion to terrorize us, always to isolate us, and to keep us in a state of uncertainty. Bad treatment, coupled with our sense of discipline as members of the Foreign Service and the Armed Forces of the United States, and the unacceptability of our captors' initial demand that the Shah be returned, ensured that, with one or two exceptions, our captors would have no real cooperation from us.

During the TWA episode, the inherent reasonableness of the initial demands of the Lebanese Shiites that their coreligionists held in Israel be returned was ultimately complied with. Furthermore, the TWA hostages were not government employees, and after they were taken off the plane, they were treated far better than we were. Thus, the Lebanese Shiites were able to generate far more empathy from most of their hostages and to draw on it for effective propaganda. The difference implies no criticism, certainly not on my part, of the leadership provided to the TWA hostages by Allyn Conwell. His "playing along" with their captors may very well have saved lives. Terrorists have learned from earlier hostage taking; they are more sophisticated and have learned how to exploit their prisoners.

Propaganda will always be one of the principal objectives of Middle East terrorism. Having this in mind, some leaders such as Prime Minister Margaret Thatcher have argued that media coverage of terrorist acts should be restricted, either by governments or by the TV networks and newspapers, in the hope that, deprived of their theater, terrorists will produce no more tragedy. Middle East terrorists know all too well that in a free society their acts have to be brought to public attention. If terrorist acts are not fully covered, terrorists will simply increase the quantum of horror to a level that compels media coverage. If the Eastern Airlines shuttle terminal at La Guardia were blown to smithereens at five o'clock one afternoon, could mention not be made of this in the press and on television? Mrs. Thatcher shares with Henry Kissinger the mistake of trying to isolate one of terrorism's many objectives. They delude themselves that they can thus deal successfully with the whole complex bundle.

In Iran, our captors' incomplete knowledge of the United States doomed their propaganda efforts from the start. But if their understanding was shallow, their bitterness over U.S. policies was deep. What many of us would concede to be serious policy errors on our part as well as the Shah's were to them the crime of the Great Satan. The Shah's White Revolution, for example, the land reform that our government had applauded, had been far from successful. When one replaces an agricultural system which works, in which typically the landlord provides land, seed, water, and motive power (i.e., bullocks) and the peasant his labor, then you have to replace the landlord. The capital assets, input, and, above all, knowledge that the peasant lacks must be supplied by other means. In Iran, as in Chile, land reform proved a disaster; peasants were not able to manage modern agricultural production and they were not trained to cope with urban industry.

Our captors referred to land reform as America's "agricultural crimes," and the industrial alternative as America's "industrial crimes." The students were familiar with the term "inappropriate technology," which was very appropriate to much of what had been introduced into Iran. While they were often mistaken on details, there was much the students told us that was essentially correct. I knew the results of promoting America's idea of what is "good" without asking the additional question about whether, in foreign circumstances, that "good" will work. Particularly disturbing was the bitter scorn with which the students referred to "human rights" and the President who had so emphatically identified himself with them. Had not Carter, after the Imperial Guard gunned down protesters in Jaleh Square in September 1978, reiterated his support for the Shah, they asked us. Carter's espousal of human rights in 1977 had excited considerable enthusiasm among the Shah's opposition in Iran. It made the Shah's government think twice, and certain repressive measures were lifted. Before long, however, the Shah's minions realized that, whatever Carter might say, human rights were not to play a role in Iranian–American relations. And they cracked down even harder.

This was the basis of the revolutionaries' fury against Carter. In their eyes, he was a hypocrite—an accusation which reflects high expectation and subsequent deep disappointment. One day, we asked Mailman what they would do if the Soviets did to Iran what they were doing to Afghanistan. "America," he replied, "would have to come to our assistance. We are too important to you." By that, Mailman meant more than strategic support. In the minds of the students, there was a continuing, underlying relationship with the United States. "One of the things we students most regret about what has happened," Mailman told us, "is that many of us will no longer be able to visit the United States." A whole generation had looked to the United States for leadership. We had moral authority, and their expectations were high. We had failed them, and their resentment was all the deeper.

Besides learning about our captors, my first six months of captivity were the occasion for self-examination, particularly my growing doubts about the Department of State. Shortcomings in the system, after all, had put our lives in jeopardy. It was easy to blame individuals. One hostage lived for the day when he could punch Henry Precht, the Country Director, in the nose. I could not blame individuals. And while still on my psychological death row, I forced myself to get rid of all thoughts about the institution. Anger debilitates, and I needed all the psychic strength and energy I could muster, if only to face my own execution. To this day, though, I have not entirely gotten over a feeling of betrayal, deepened by a lifetime commitment to a Foreign Service career. In a recurring nightmare, the Department of State has loaded us on a plane and sent us back to resume our captivity. I see the familiar faces of the students welcoming us. Trying from captivity to convey these feelings to my family at home, while at the same time not providing propaganda for my captors, was not easy. On January 9, 1980, in my first letter to Mark, my oldest son, I cited Thomas à Kempis's *Imitation of Christ*: "A man does well if he does the will of the community and not his own will." Then I commented. "But what *is* the will of my community? Is it my employer? If so, it has landed me in a most awkward predicament."

As our captivity continued, I recognized that I could not be too critical of a branch of government in which I had played an active role. From that, I reasoned that all of us, hostages, student captors, and U.S. government, were responsible. Granted that our stakes and perceptions were very different, and that tough negotiations would be required before we ever got out, it did little good to say, "It's all your fault." It was *our* problem. Little in a career of bureaucratic infighting had prepared me for such understanding.

April brought peaceful days. Each time we were taken to the back yard of the Residence for exercise, spring was more in evidence and the air had a softer quality. Nature seemed to reinforce the Easter message that life renews. Not long before Easter, Ahmad, Mailman's deputy, came to our room and asked me to accompany him. I was blindfolded, as usual, and led to the Ambassador's suite, where a table had been pulled out from the wall. American clergy were coming to minister to us at Easter, Ahmad explained. The guards would have to set up a communion table. Would I show them how it should be arranged? I had discussed comparative religion, Islam and Christianity, with some of my guards. As far as they were concerned, I was the house liturgist.

On Easter, we were led downstairs, and when we were told to remove the towels covering our faces, we found ourselves outside the library. There stood Mailman, bowing like a majordomo, an ironic smile on his face. Inside, Tooth presided over a mixed scene: students, most of them armed; three clergymen; a table bearing the communion elements; cookies and candies on plates; and dominating it all, TV lights and whirring cameras. Throughout the service, the cameras would zoom in on us.

We sat down and studied the clergymen. From his vestments, one was clearly a Catholic priest. He introduced himself as Father Darrell Rupiper. Two others, the Reverends Jack Bremer and Nelson Thompson, were either Baptist or Methodist. One of the ministers preached a short sermon, then launched into the communion prayer. At this point he was interrupted by Father Rupiper. "We have a joint ministry," he reminded the other, and the minister quickly apologized. Rupiper then gave his own short sermon, not very different from what we had just heard. I winced at their content: we should love our enemies. It was sound Christian doctrine, but was hardly the way to get through to angry hostages. In general conversation, these clergy were even worse. "Gee, fellas, I would sure like to spend twenty days with you," said Father Rupiper to one group of hostages. "It would give me a wonderful chance to meditate."

Being rather high-church Episcopalian, I gravitated to the priest rather than to the other two clergymen, and tried to tell him something of my spiritual progress in captivity. He was clearly not interested and suggested that I talk to one of the other ministers. I sensed that the underlying motive of this group was not primarily pastoral. They were peace activists out to make a political case for our captors. I did not know at the time the extent to which this priest was not dissimilar from some of the politicized clergy with whom, after my release, I was to have problems.

By mid-April, we had word that the Shah was in Cairo and dying. When on April 25, 1980, we heard through our windows the funereal "March from Saul," and popular rejoicing, we assumed him to be beyond human extradition; the ostensible reason for our continued captivity was gone. Around this time, some of us had begun to run out of patience with Larry. We had gotten on well until, in February, we were given permission to talk. It was a great relief, but it also brought trouble. Relations deteriorated to the point where I had spoken to Ahmad about finding us another roommate. When on April 25 Ahmad poked his head in through our door at four in the afternoon to tell us to pack our things, we thought this was a tactful way to separate us from Larry. It was only after trips to the washroom disclosed that everyone's gear was stacked in the hallway, ready for shipment, that we realized the move was not due to Larry.

As darkness fell, with flashbulbs going off outside our window, and the noise of cars driving up, we began to think the students were taking our "graduation" pictures before sending us home. Then we heard a sound which, once heard, is unforgettable, of handcuffs being snapped on. Perhaps the students were observing full security right up to the end. We found ourselves in a car, with blankets over our heads, handcuffed together. If the car went downhill, I thought, it would be taking us to the airport, and home. But we went uphill, obviously toward north Tehran. I was helped out of the car, a student removed my blanket, then checked off my name. Before us was a long, dirty room full of military bunks. I was still handcuffed to Larry.

Our removal and dispersal was the consequence of the aborted helicopter rescue mission. The funeral music that had so misled us was for the American airmen killed on the mission. After our return to the United States, I talked to Gary Sick, who served on the National Security Council staff throughout our captivity, and is the author of *All Fall Down,* the standard book on the hostage crisis as seen from Washington. "Look," he pointed out, "you had been held for nearly six months. Your guards by then were bored and probably sleepy. Our people would have gotten in with stun grenades . . ." I interrupted him: "How did you know the guards were bored and sleepy? In fact, the week before the rescue attempt, security consciousness among the guards was at its peak. If one of us was suspected of looking out into the corridor, much less outside, there was hell to pay. They even painted our washroom window, evidently after a perimeter guard had seen a face peeking out. I remember, because I helped steady the ladder while Ahmad did the painting." "That was gracious of you," Sick commented. I replied that, among our captors, Ahmad was one of the more helpful ones. No use having him fall off a ladder. "From hindsight," I resumed, "it is clear that the students were aware that our people had observers in the high-rise buildings around the compound, trying to identify us. In February, Hossein Sheikholeslam had warned us: 'We hope that Mr. Carter will do nothing foolish like a helicopter rescue attempt, for we are ready for it, and some if not all of you will be killed.' Don't you think, if everyone in Washington knew that Mr. Carter was running out of options, the students might have arrived at the same conclusion and taken precautions accordingly?" Just because they are Middle Easterners, I might have added, does not mean that they cannot think as clearly as we.

The dispersal point in north Tehran was a rich man's villa, obviously abandoned in a hurry. Kupke and I took bunks at one end of a long room, while Larry, very isolated, took the other end. After several days, a guard announced that Kupke would leave that night for parts unknown. I did not look forward to being stuck with Larry. Then a more junior guard, whom we had tutored in English, took advantage of Larry's absence in the washroom to observe pointedly that Larry "is being very quiet these days." Kupke and I nodded. We understood each other. The junior guard left the room, and soon the senior guard returned. Larry, he said, was to depart that night in Kupke's place.

Shortly, Kupke and I began our progress through Iran, winding up, after four moves, with others in a confiscated villa in Isfahan, until mid-August, when all the hostages were reassembled in a political prison in Tehran. Our dispersal was a miserable time, not only because of feelings of abandonment but because human relations do not stand up well under the harsh and confining conditions in which we lived that summer. One of the questions put to me on the lecture circuit is: "Do you continue to see your fellow hostages?" My answer: "With some exceptions, no." In a combat platoon, whose members grow to depend on each other, comradeship develops. However hellish the combat, the men welcome reunions because of the bonds forged by their mutual reliance. But we, with nothing to do, simply exhausted each other's company. At our reunion at the Greenbrier three months after our release, roommate avoidance was much in evidence. Another former hostage told me rather grimly, "There we were at the White House, being cheered as heroes. I looked down the line and I could pick out the clay feet in every hostage." I could see his point. I was certainly aware of my own clay feet.

Yet even Isfahan had its compensations. The students liked to give us religious books, one of which was by the Dutch evangelist Corrie Ten Boom, who had been imprisoned by the Nazis for helping Dutch Jews to escape. As she describes stuffing her few pathetic possessions into a pillowcase when she is to be moved to another prison, I had a shock of recognition. We, too, used pillowcases when we were moved. And I realized that we had earned our way into a goodly fellowship, of those who unjustly had had to "do time" because of what they stood for. More importantly, it was a time of intense personal introspection and focus, which, after my release, I was determined to share with others.

I now understood, too, why so many of these people had used prison as an opportunity to write. For example, St. Paul. How often in his writings do we encounter jail metaphors: "a prisoner of the Lord"; "an emissary in chains"! How much of the Christian faith was in fact shaped by his prison experience? And Cervantes, who conceived Don Quixote while serving as a Moorish galley slave. And Marco Polo, who dictated his *Travels* while a prisoner of war of the Genoese. And Henri Pirenne, the great Belgian economic historian of the Middle Ages, who did his greatest work, without notes, while a German prisoner of war. I could hardly put myself in their class. But their example encouraged me to write, even though I knew the manuscript might well be seized, as indeed it was, but I knew, too, that what I had begun in captivity, ripened over time, would someday find a readership.

On December 18, we were moved from the political prison to a guesthouse. By contrast, it was luxury—our own bathroom, and windows we could look out of. The reason for the move to better quarters was explained by the visit on Christmas Day of the Algerian Ambassador and some of his staff. In French, while the students glowered, I told him not to be too favorably impressed, that we had been in the guesthouse hardly a week. We were still in the guesthouse on January 19, 1981, when Algerian doctors examined us and we were allowed to look at newspapers for the first time. As they put on our blindfolds, still required for any movement outside of our rooms, the guards joked about it. That afternoon, we had individually been taken in for talks with Ahmad. Some of you, he said, are being sent home tomorrow. You are all about to be interviewed for television, where you will give your impressions of your captivity. His plain implication was that those who cooperated and said the correct things would be on the first list.

In the next room, I found some of our guards. Next to the cameras sat Mary (Nilofar Ebtaker), who had interviewed me before. She asked me what my impressions were. I looked at Ali, Little Dwarf, and Abbas, and said what fine service they had rendered. Her face lit up. Obviously, I was a hostage she could work with. She asked me what conclusions I had drawn. Never, I said, no matter how serious your grievance against a foreign government, should you take over an Embassy, for an Embassy is a means by which nations communicate and preserve the peace. Mary's face froze, and I was led out of the TV room, thinking for sure I would be on list B.

None of us slept well that last night. Planes normally take off from Mehrabad around seven in the morning. From four on, we waited for the students to give us a sign. Daybreak stretched into morning, morning into afternoon. We knew that the mandate would pass from Carter to Reagan at 12:30 p.m., Washington time. Would Reagan cancel the negotiations that we knew were in progress? I had begun to resign myself to remaining in captivity, when a student entered our room. "All right, let's go." "Where?" we asked. "You're going home." We looked at each other, and no one said a word; we had had too many disappointments. Blindfolded, we were loaded into a van, which headed downhill. When we were told to take our blindfolds off, we could see the plane on the tarmac, just ahead of us. But it wasn't until we were safely on the Algerian airliner that we let go.

I am not a backslapper. Amid the hoopla, and trying to remember names, I found an empty seat and waited. Larry and I shook hands. I greeted Sam. I had not seen either for some time. Nor had I seen Ann Swift, with whom I now had a quiet chat. "Well, Mike," said Bruce Laingen, "I guess this was more than the three months you bargained for." I asked the stewardess when they would start serving champagne. As soon, she said, as we cleared Iranian airspace. We took off, and before long, I was drinking a toast to myself in good, if non-vintage, Veuve Clicquot.

7 / REENTRY
AND RETIREMENT

OUR AIRCRAFT LANDED at Algiers Airport, where a reception awaited us. I found myself working the room, rather ponderously, in my best French, telling various Algerian officials what a grand job they had done. I was trying, very consciously, to fit myself back into my Foreign Service role. At the same time I had a creeping awareness that it wasn't going to work, then or ever.

After scarcely more than an hour, we boarded two U.S. Air Force planes for Rhein-Main Air Force Base in Germany, en route to the Air Force hospital in Wiesbaden. On the plane, I talked to Sheldon Krys, today Ambassador to Trinidad and Tobago, who then was the executive director of the Bureau of Near East and South Asian Affairs; he was a warm and effective friend to Louisa and the other hostages' families. To my horror, he told me that former President Jimmy Carter was on his way to Wiesbaden to join us. I told Sheldon of the hostages' negative feelings about Carter, of one roommate who during a discussion in which I had tried to defend some of the President's actions had shouted, "Don't listen to this man! Anyone who defends Carter has to be sick!"

Almost desperately, I asked Sheldon if there was any way to delay Carter's arrival, perhaps a layover en route, at least until the hostages had their initial psychological checkups and time to regain a sense of perspective. Sheldon said he doubted it, and then went up and down the aircraft aisle, talking to my colleagues. Upon Carter's arrival—though I did not know this at the time—he warned Carter that the hostages might not feel about him the way he felt about the hostages. Sheldon even forecast, with accuracy, the hostile questions Mr. Carter would be asked, and in what order, beginning with the government's decision to admit the Shah. Carter's initial reception by the hostages went as I had expected. After the reception line broke up, I went into the adjacent room, where batteries of telephones had been set up for direct calls home. I paused for a moment, before calling my family, to exchange a few words with former Vice-President Walter Mondale. But I broke off the conversation, perhaps too abruptly, saying that I wanted to call home. Mr. Mondale gave me a quizzical look. Perhaps, I thought as I headed toward an empty phone booth, he is only just realizing that he isn't Vice-President any longer.

Then President Carter came in and walked past me, heading for the telephone booths. Most hostages were making their second or third call home. The initial euphoria was over, and I wondered what marital or other problems might be coming over the wires. Carter stopped at one booth and took the receiver out of the hand of an astonished hostage. "Now," he said into the phone, a big grin on his face, "guess who *this* is." And he repeated this performance all around the room. In retrospect, I am perhaps too critical of a man Louisa and others had grown to admire, and who cared very much about the hostages. As I was to remind countless lecture audiences —if the taking and holding of the hostages was a humiliation, the negotiations that Carter inspired were a victory. During the TWA hostage crisis, President Reagan, for all his campaign criticism of Carter's handling of our hostage situation, followed much the same negotiating path. We, however, had suffered as a result of Carter's fatal flaw, which manifested itself in so many other ways—his trying to have it both ways. One cannot keep a large and growing Embassy in Tehran for the purpose of improving relations with a revolution and then give shelter, whatever the reason, to the object of the revolution, its archenemy.

Wiesbaden quickly became a laboratory and we the guinea pigs. The medical staff had not known what psychological shape we would be in and were prepared for the worst. Even though we seemed to be physically fit, both tests and observations showed that our stress levels were unusually high. The psychiatrists were faced with a daunting problem. They had to find ways to alert us that the months ahead might not be easy. At the same time, with the hostages pressing to go home, and without the time for them to develop self-awareness, the doctors had to say certain things flat out. My shrink was Esther Roberts, M.D., Deputy Assistant Secretary for Mental Health Programs in the Department of State, who became a good friend. "You might have to divorce Louisa," she said quietly. It was, to me, a bit blunt. "Why?" I asked. I knew that Louisa had asked that Esther be assigned to me. "Because Louisa is so famous. She has been in every living room and bedroom in the United States on TV. As for you, well, I mean, you're just one of the hostages." I was furious. I knew what a superb job Louisa had done on television. And suddenly it occurred to me that I might be just as able to do so. Outside the hospital, we could see the television cameras, their crews hoping for a glimpse of the hostages. I went out for a walk and approached the cameras. Instantly recognized, I experienced the soon-to-be-familiar sensation of microphones thrust at me.

Why did I feel the need to compete with Louisa? Our marriage always had that element in it. But Esther had put her finger on something deeper, my feelings of hostility, which I did not accept for several years and which can easily arise when people suddenly find their lives beyond their control. One day in the last weeks of our captivity, a roommate had launched an attack on FLAG, the Family Liaison Action Group of which Louisa was vice-president and spokesperson. "Here they are, gallivanting all over Europe talking to heads of government." He was referring to the mission led by Louisa which had been received by President Valéry Giscard d'Estaing of France and Prime Minister Margaret Thatcher, among others. He had added: "They're all having a great time on the strength of what is happening to us, while we suffer." I had, rather diplomatically I thought, asked him to reserve judgment until we all got home. After our release, another roommate who had joined in the attack apologized to me. But what I did not recognize in Iran was the extent to which I, deep down, shared the resentment. Or that our families, too, had experienced hostile feelings toward us. Prisoners of war returning from Vietnam and their families had the same problem.

Our stay in Wiesbaden lasted five days. As I got off the plane at Stewart Air Force Base, en route to West Point, there they were, Louisa and the four boys, my youngest now several inches taller than I. I had not seen them for sixteen months. I was home. The full impact of reentry, however, was delayed by public hoopla, which actually was rather fun. I had never expected to be seated next to New York's Mayor Koch riding up Broadway waving to a cheering crowd in a blizzard of ticker tape. With Bruce Laingen in Washington suffering from laryngitis, I gave the speech on the steps of City Hall on behalf of the hostages. In April came another memorable moment as I marched with Louisa down Fifth Avenue, led by the police commissioner and followed by hundreds of New York's finest, members of the Holy Name Society of the police precincts of Manhattan, the Bronx, and Staten Island. Behind us, the pipe band wailed "The Wearing of the Green." It was like the St. Patrick's Day of our New York childhoods come to life. We wheeled and without breaking step marched into St. Patrick's Cathedral for mass. "You see," Cardinal Cooke said to Louisa, "I told you you'd get him back." All heady stuff, and without attaching too much importance to it, I throve on it. The Foreign Service had often thrust me into temporary roles which it expected me to play.

Hoopla kept reality at bay. It was just what I needed at the time. Yet, during that period of suspended animation, I managed to lay some important foundations in my thinking. Addressing the Holy Name Society communion breakfast at the Hilton, I concluded: "We had lost our moral authority in Iran, and for that, more than fifty hostages had to suffer. And so, too, with the cop on the beat. He can have all the backup, the squad cars, the computer banks, but once he has lost his moral authority with those he has sworn to protect, he is worse than useless." As I finished, Commissioner McGuire leaped up and grasped my hand. "That's it," he said, "moral authority. That's what I keep telling them . . ." But I was thinking about the United States as a self-constituted policeman as well as a self-appointed model and financier of the developing world and how, with the taking of our Embassy, that world was turning against us.

Another foundation, laid soon after my return, was the full realization that I could handle television. Lecturing I knew I could do. The need to master a childhood stutter had drawn me to the study of foreign languages and also to public speaking. As an enlisted man in the Army, I had volunteered to give the weekly TI and E (troop information and education) lectures to more than a thousand troops about to go on pass. But

I had no real experience with television. In fact, I rarely watched it. Yet, the day after our arrival at West Point, I found myself being driven in what I learned to call a limo, across the frozen countryside of upstate New York, to be interviewed by ABC's Barbara Walters. I entered the split-level house that she had borrowed for the occasion. Just inside the front door, on the landing, stood a small woman obviously wondering how she would handle a newly released hostage whose behavior might be somewhat erratic. She posed the first question, and I began to speak, quoting easily from my confiscated manuscript. Ms. Walters was too experienced to interrupt me unnecessarily.

The social adjustments I had to make were not onerous. I soon realized when I was talking too much or making too many cocky statements. Louisa and I faced some obvious problems. When I first called her from Wiesbaden and had trouble locating her, she had explained: "There are so many calls from the media—I had to leave my house." I exploded with anger. "What do you mean, *my* house? I paid for that house. I laid out that garden." But in effect, in sixteen months, she had learned to live alone and manage independently. On our first night home in Washington, it rained heavily. The next morning, I got behind the wheel of the Subaru to drive to the Department, but the car wouldn't start. Louisa turned to me angrily. "That car started perfectly the whole time you were away."

Several years later, I was a guest lecturer and teacher at the Nichols School in Buffalo, New York. The class had been reading the *Odyssey* and had reached the point where Penelope realizes that her husband, Ulysses, is really home from Troy after a ten-year absence. At that point she gets furious with him. To the class, I reconstructed what Penelope might have said: "Off you went. Big deal. Never really asked me. Left me alone to cope. Now you barge back in here. Take over.

Just who do you think you are, anyway?" It is only when one resumes a marriage that one sees who has been doing what. I found sixteen monthly bank statements in a neat pile, all unopened, awaiting my return. In other matters where "turf" had been reassigned, we sometimes collided. Moreover, my rigorous suppression, throughout the captivity, of my sexual instincts was not exactly helpful to our marriage, but these in time recovered, along with everything else. We both had changed. I overheard Louisa say at a dinner party, "One Mike Kennedy went out to Tehran, and another came back." I listened, fascinated, as she went on: "I think I like the one that came back even better."

Recovery from the hostage experience, for both Louisa and myself, became an important, although not the only, factor in my decision about remaining in the Foreign Service. The Department made every effort to help us reestablish our careers. The director general of the Foreign Service flew out to Wiesbaden to discuss possible future assignments. When we came home, however, there was no pressure, and no deadline on career decisions. Personnel made the first move, at the end of a day late in February. Louisa and I were at home, sitting on our bed, when the telephone rang. Would I be interested in serving as economic counselor in Brasília? The biggest "econ" job in Latin America, it was at least as important as the many assignments as Deputy Chief of Mission for which, I learned, I was also being considered. Had the offer been made in October 1979, I would have leaped with excitement. Now it left me appreciative but indifferent. Captivity had given me a glimpse of the other side of the mountain, where the sticks and carrots of a Foreign Service career, as well as its substantial challenges, no longer seemed to matter all that much. Not unimportantly, I had celebrated my fiftieth birthday three months before, which meant, given all my years of government service, that I could retire any time I chose, at fifty percent of my pay.

I had my own reasons for irritation with Personnel. In order to flesh out my performance file, for I had accomplished nothing in fourteen months of captivity, I submitted letters of thanks and commendation which I had received for my media work immediately after our return—from Barbara Walters, from Ambassador Shlaudeman in Buenos Aires for a broadcast in Spanish, from Ambassador Hartman in Paris for one in French. And many others. A much-embarrassed personnel officer informed me that none of these was acceptable, because they mentioned Louisa. To protect Foreign Service wives who chose to lead their own lives, and not be pressured on a two-for-the-price-of-one basis to serve as unpaid adjuncts to their husbands' careers, no personnel record could ever mention a spouse. It was a good rule, to which, however, an exception might have been made in these unusual circumstances. But none was.

More important even than the attraction of any new assignment was my growing loss of confidence in the system. Upon my return, I was impressed by the extent to which the Department had accepted that it might not have had all the answers to the Iranian crisis. The Bureau of Intelligence and Research was reaching out, as never before, to academia, sponsoring seminars, in which I met Nikki Keddie and other Iran specialists. But, apart from the widening of its peripheral vision, the system had not gone further in examining itself, to ask why it had been so slow in assessing the reasons for the collapse of the Shah's government and, more inexcusably, for the takeover of the Embassy. A number of the returning hostages had hoped that our experience would generate a major inquiry, perhaps by a blue-ribbon panel of distinguished Americans, into the causes of our debacle in Iran. Such an inquiry would begin with the more immediate and obvious causes, but it would go much further. Henry Precht, for example, had said, over coffee following our return: "We put too much on the Shah." Henry had been as prescient about what was to happen to the Shah as he had been wrong about what was to happen to us. Now he was making a very serious point indeed, one with implications that went beyond the fall of the Shah and the takeover of the Embassy, to the very way our government manages its foreign business.

If we had put too many demands on the Shah, it was because there was inadequate central authority to monitor and assess the demands of powerful single-interest agencies in Washington, each of which saw Iran in terms of its own parochial view; each agency was prepared to go to the mat with other agencies to ensure that its requirements were met. Thus, the Central Intelligence Agency demanded electronic-intelligence facilities vital for monitoring possible Soviet nuclear testing; Treasury, among others, demanded Iranian cooperation in oil pricing; the Drug Enforcement Administration wanted cooperation in narcotics control; powerful business interests as well as the Department of Commerce wanted priority for U.S. corporations to win contracts for prestigious and profitable projects such as telecommunications. Given our balance-of-payments problems in the 1970s, the Shah's desire to buy the latest U.S. military equipment, besides its strategic implications, helped Treasury to repatriate dollars. Moreover, foreign sales helped to spread overhead costs. Thus, the unit cost of such equipment to the U.S. Armed Forces could be lowered. Woe betide any U.S. Ambassador who did not deliver what each agency demanded.

Since the Shah made all major decisions, no American requests stood a chance unless his demands were also met. So a mutual dependency grew, and we, over time, became identified with his misallocation of resources, the corruption of his regime, as well as the torture, imprisonment, and executions he was responsible for. Many items on our request list—for example, drug control—were indeed worthy. However, we lacked broader goals against which short-term interests and the dependencies they engendered could be assessed and given due priority. The Shah demanded and we accepted that there be no official contact with dissidents, such as the mullahs. As a result, as Hossein Sheikholeslam reminded us bitterly in our basement room: "You Americans saw only the elite." Later I was told that the Central Intelligence Agency had considered a parallel program designed to keep in touch with the dissidents while its representatives under Embassy and other official cover cooperated with the government of the Shah. But nothing came of it. American officials tended to see Iran as the Shah and his minions wanted it seen, missing portents that by 1977 were becoming clear to observers not wearing official blinders. The Shah himself went into exile bitterly critical of the Americans for not warning him of the extent to which he was losing his own people.

Had a blue-ribbon panel not been willing to investigate and take on our whole system of foreign-affairs management, it could at least have pointed out the flaws that had led directly to the disaster in Iran and have noted their implications for future relations with the Middle East. But no inquiry ever took place. Shortly before my return, Louisa asked a senior official whether there might be such an inquiry, and he replied: "The important thing now is to protect careers." When I raised the possibility with someone else, the reply was "Oh, God, not another Who-lost-Iran." Memories of Senator Joseph McCarthy and what happened to the careers of those China hands who correctly foresaw the communist takeover of 1949 linger on. How much worse if an investigation had brought to light how incorrect certain officers had been in their estimate of what was happening in Iran.

In March 1981, I delivered a speech before the Iran–American Business Council in which I spelled out some of the reasons why, in my estimation, the Embassy had been taken over and why we had been so unprepared for it. Arthur was among the guests. Afterward, he came up to me. "Gee, Mike, I don't want to criticize what was a fine presentation, but you needn't be so hard on yourself. After all, we had every right to be in Iran. The Provisional Government had every duty to protect us." Right? Duty? By whose standard? Had he, had the Department, learned nothing from the experience? All I could do was disagree. To which Arthur added, curtly: "Well, if you want to talk about it, that means washing our dirty linen in public." So the coverup was under way. Tehran was to be considered an aberration, unlikely to be repeated, and not an early warning of the need to change our relations with the Third World. Unlike the TWA passengers, who were carefully debriefed in Wiesbaden about their captors, no one seemed to want to know even the names of ours. We finally were able to get a short debriefing, on April 13, by the Bureau of Intelligence and Research.

As if to symbolize the burial of unpleasant memories, also on April 13 there was an awards ceremony in the main auditorium of the Department of State, ostensibly for the hostages. Secretary of State Alexander Haig was late. As the U.S. Marine Corps Band thumped its way through most of its repertory, we waited. Finally he showed up, only to tell us that "we," the Reagan Administration, would have handled the hostage crisis very differently. In due course, he pinned the Medal of Valor on the chargé, the rest of the hostages being told that since the Secretary was running late, we could pick up our medals in room 1308. But by then everyone remotely connected with the hostage crisis had received some kind of prize. And so we hostages saw coming up to the stage the former Country Director for Iran, Henry Precht. As he joined us on the stage, red-faced, he had the grace to turn his head, so he would not have to look us in the eye. Then he was given the Superior Honor Award. The Foreign Service was closing ranks. Everyone had done just a super job, no questions asked or conclusions drawn. After that, in 1983, two Embassy chanceries in Beirut were destroyed by terrorists.

By the end of March, I was beginning to conclude that until the Foreign Service begins to probe and rethink much of its received wisdom, to analyze its own conceptual blinders, and to reduce the constraints that its system imposes on the considerable talent it has at its disposal, it will continue to disappoint the expectations that the American people have of it. Outsiders will continue to think that they can do just as good a job. And the Foreign Service cannot complain when, increasingly, senior jobs which belong to the Foreign Service are given to political appointees, a process which backs up the promotional system and undercuts morale. But if, as I believe, the Foreign Service could not reform itself, if pressures for change must come from the outside, then outside was perhaps where I could make a greater contribution.

Immediately after the awards ceremony, a number of us hostages repaired to the Greenbrier, the great West Virginia resort, for our only reunion. The keynote speech was given by Martin Symonds, a psychiatrist who was an adviser to the New York Police Department and who specialized in the effects of violence. "Each of you has been through a death-threatening experience," he said. "Before captivity, the self that you thought you were in fact was the imaginary self, the kind of person certain to make ambassador or whatever goal you might have set for yourself. But there you were, facing possible execution, and suddenly none of these goals had very much relevance. Other things did. And so, possibly for the first time, you caught a glimpse of your real self, what you are. You might not like that real self. But don't ever let go of it. Cultivate it. For that is the self you are going to have to live with and someday die with." I recognized everything he was saying.

Shortly after the keynote speech, we broke up into small groups. Mine was led by the medical director of the Department of State, Jerome Korschak, an internist, not a psychiatrist. "I'm tired of seeing you hostages running around making speeches here, getting awards there. When are you going to settle down, get back to work?" That thought really set him off. "You've got to get back in the rut—in the rut. That's where you all belong. That's where your recovery will lie." I raised my hand. "We just got through hearing the keynote speaker," I said, "whom presumably you selected to speak to us. He just made an important distinction, between our real and our imaginary selves. Now, what is the work that you want us to get back to? In the bureaucracy, people are known quantities. They are assigned jobs for which their qualifications are established. We would hope to get the kind of jobs we had before, at a slightly higher level. Now, we developed those qualifications based on the aspirations we had then and the people we were then, but suppose, as the keynoter just said, these aspirations, thanks to a death-threatening experience, have changed? Shouldn't we take some time before crawling back into the rut, to find out who we really are now, and what our proper rut should be?"

The psychiatrists in the room were exchanging amused glances. Between them and this internist, as I learned, there was little love lost. I was already convinced that the old rut was not for me. An exciting new possibility had opened up, outside government, which seemed to offer just what I was looking for, the development of the potential that the Foreign Service, I felt, had never really tapped. And Arthur's stricture about "washing our dirty linen in public" was very much to the point. In all decency, I could not remain in the State Department and at the same time criticize its methods and its management of American foreign relations generally, and I felt that I had a lot to say. My field of endeavor would no longer be the structure of foreign-affairs management but public opinion, to which, ultimately, foreign-affairs management has to respond.

And so the day came, in May 1981, when I picked up the telephone and dialed Personnel. Then I put the receiver down. I thought of twenty-one years, of the moment when, as a Third Secretary calling officially at the Yemeni Foreign Ministry, I first realized that I was representing the United States of America. I thought of the extraordinary ability of my colleagues, their decency, which made work with so many of them a pleasure. And the fun of being included in a foreign society, the thrill of being "in the know" when great events are taking place, and of making a contribution to them. And my bitterness over our betrayal, over the frustration of bureaucracy, the inanities of the personnel system? Esther Roberts's cautionary words came back to me as I held the telephone. "Don't forget that the family members who got along least well with the departed are those who grieve most at the funeral. Don't quit unless you have something else that you really want to do." I did. I had received an offer that was hard to refuse. I picked up the telephone again, very reluctantly, dialed Personnel, and with confidence told them that I planned to retire in August from the Foreign Service.

8 / THE AYATOLLAH
IN THE CATHEDRAL

"AND DID He, too, not experience fear? Obviously. And anger?
. . . And doubt? . . . And as each of us goes through a crisis,
that is our Lent . . . How we cope with crisis, how we overcome our weakness, that is our Easter." It was March 15,
1981, and I was preaching at the Cathedral Church of St.
John the Divine, in New York City. I had met the Dean of
the Cathedral, the Very Reverend James Parks Morton, at the
breakfast at the Tavern-on-the-Green before Mayor Koch's
ticker-tape parade for the hostages in January, and he had
invited me to preach. As I came down from the pulpit, the
Dean said, "Why, Mike, you were preaching the Gospel!"
Only later was I to appreciate the irony of that remark.

Before very long, the Dean was calling me in Washington
nearly every morning, unrelenting in his efforts to woo me
away from the Foreign Service. His offer, made on April 2,
was twofold—to be paid director of my own foreign-affairs
institute at the Cathedral and, on a volunteer basis, together
with Louisa, to chair the capital campaign committee. The
Cathedral was about to launch a fund-raising drive to complete its two towers, and to add to its endowment. Neither

Louisa nor I had any fund-raising experience, but that, we were told, was not important. While not wealthy ourselves, Louisa and I were New York-born and well-introduced into the Episcopalian families which, in the past, had been the mainstay of the Cathedral's successive building campaigns. It was assumed that our hostage-related visibility would help us increase an awareness of the Cathedral and its needs and rekindle traditional interest and support.

For someone looking for a way out of the Foreign Service, the offer came at just the right moment. I felt that I had paid my dues to my country. Now it was time to repay my debt to Him who had led me out of the house of bondage. Morton's superior, the Episcopal Bishop of New York, the Right Reverend Paul Moore, Jr., joined in the recruitment effort. "You can't keep on talking just about the hostage experience," he told me. "We can offer you a platform." The Cathedral itself was not without attraction. On Morningside Heights, the city's highest point of land, and only a few blocks from Columbia University, it is the principal landmark on Manhattan's Upper West Side. Although its fund-raising work, under the honorary chairmanship of President Reagan, has since been taken over by powerful real-estate interests engaged in high-cost development, in 1981 the Cathedral still placed highest priority on the needs of its Hispanic and black environment. It had encouraged "sweat-equity," the restoration of deteriorating buildings by their tenants, and thereby the preservation of mixed and low-income neighborhoods. Most appealing, perhaps, was the stoneyard next to the Cathedral, where apprentices, largely from ghetto areas, were already cutting stone for the towers, reviving skills that had all but disappeared in the United States. "We are building a statement in stone of our faith!" the Dean told us. On a different level, musical programs and other events in its vast premises had made the Cathedral known as a public forum. It could become, I thought, a center for serious discussion of the role of religion in international affairs.

By the end of April 1981, I had accepted the Dean's offer, and for a while the hostage spotlight was turned on the Cathedral and its building plans. Louisa and I rented the lower floors of a brownstone on the Upper East Side, midway between where we each had been brought up. My retirement from the Foreign Service having become effective August 22, the Cathedral Peace Institute opened for business on September 1, 1981. I had one assistant, Marie Moser, and a substantial Cathedral staff to help when necessary.

From the beginning, I felt that we needed an event to differentiate my approach to peace from that of the many organizations that used that complex word so indiscriminately, and to establish the identity and credibility of the Cathedral Peace Institute. Along these lines, the Cathedral Peace Institute sponsored a conference in April 1982 on "Violence: Is Religion Its Cause or Its Cure?"—to which we brought scholars from Cairo, Jerusalem, and Northern Ireland. Muhammad Shaalan, M.D., an Egyptian psychiatrist, and Hassan Hanafi, an Egyptian theologian, debated the nature and future of Islamic fundamentalism. Hanafi argued that Islam, truly resurgent, was an "unstoppable trend." No movement based in the secular West could survive any longer in the Muslim world. Therefore, he maintained, all the present-day so-called Muslim rulers who did not govern on the basis of the Sharia, of Islamic law, were illegitimate. But, he asked, given the rigidities of Islamic law, how could you build political entities capable of dealing with Western states and meeting the challenge of today? Shaalan argued that, on the contrary, Islam is not really resurgent but is only being used by other forces. Islamic fundamentalism is an act of desperation. Hence the terrorist acts of the fundamentalists are partly the death throes of a dying religion, partly an effort to assure themselves that Islam will never die. It is not a movement that is progressive, Shaalan concluded; it reflects a search for certainty in a time of uncertainty, a cloak for frustration and violence.

Impressive, too, was the contribution of Jehoshaphat Harkabi, the former Israeli major general, an academic, and the author of *The Bar Kokhba Syndrome*, who had retired from his post as director of military intelligence following disagreements with Menachem Begin. Commenting on the influence of religion on adventurist tendencies in Israeli foreign policy, he described the Messiah complex—"that we can commit any imbecility and a Messiah, the United States, will always come to our rescue." Because of that illusion, he noted, Israel did not exercise the prudence that any nation, and particularly one in Israel's difficult situation, should.

Although the conference on religion and violence was our major event at the Cathedral, perhaps even more significant were the preaching and lecturing I did around the country, for which the Cathedral Peace Institute was the launching pad. To our dismay, however, I quickly began to see problems at the Cathedral. Essentially, it was an entertainment center. The absence of serious commitment to the Christian faith and its demands, coupled with circus-like spectaculars such as tightrope walking in the nave, and added to the Cathedral's confused management, also put off potential donors among New York's Episcopalians. The capital campaign for which we were the chair never got off the ground.

Moreover, what I most feared when I established the Cathedral Peace Institute soon came to pass. Its name had not been of my choosing, since I was well aware of the negative connotations the word "peace" brings to mind for many people. When the Dean at length prevailed upon me to accept it, I obtained his assurance that the word "peace" would not necessarily imply or require me to express my position on nuclear disarmament or arms control. Then as now, my view is that, apart from the critical moral dimension, the technical and diplomatic questions of arms control were beyond the competence of churches. Such matters properly pertain to the state. More than that, I had every reason to think that if arms control became an issue within the churches to the point where I would have to take a stand, I was bound to come out with something intensely displeasing to my ecclesiastical employers. I was by no means an expert on arms control, but my responsibilities in Athens had included NATO affairs, and arms control issues had been part of my course at the National War College. What little I knew had a wider and deeper range than the smattering and nattering I was beginning to hear from many church and peace people.

When I first came to the Cathedral, in September 1981, nuclear disarmament was not high on the agenda of the public. What populist activity there was was largely centered at Riverside Church, the Cathedral's neighbor on Morningside Heights. In November 1981, I received an invitation to lunch with the Reverend William Sloane Coffin, who had ministered to the hostages in Tehran. With us was his associate, Cora Weiss, like Coffin a veteran of the Vietnam anti-war movement and, in her case, very much to the political left. Over pâté and red wine, they told me that their nuclear-disarmament campaign was going nowhere. Nobody seemed interested; and they suggested that if someone with my visibility and credibility, buttressed by my newly established Cathedral Peace Institute, were to take a leading role, I might give their campaign the impetus it needed. My wish to avoid disarmament issues, along with what I knew of Ms. Weiss's politics, made me reject the offer out of hand. I told them that I had my own avenue to explore, of educating the public to think more cogently about foreign affairs so that it could enjoy a more effective influence on government. Coffin did not like being turned down. "You're going to explore all that academic stuff? We're offering you action!" Two months later, I had action aplenty, as groups of extreme peace activists began their efforts to silence me.

In January 1982, for example, during a preaching tour under the auspices of the Episcopal Diocese of Southern Ohio, where I was addressing the topic "Living as a Christian in an Unjust World," I was trailed by a team of extreme peace activists determined to disrupt my sermons. They had learned the trick of non-stop, staccato, interruptive speech, designed to deny the lecturer the opportunity to maintain the initiative. In March 1982, at Fairmount Presbyterian Church in Cleveland Heights, an obviously well-briefed heckler began: "Okay, Moorhead, let's look at the record, h'm? Where have you served—Yemen, Lebanon, Chile! What does that suggest, Moorhead?" Before he was able to convince the stunned congregation that I was at least James Bond, I broke in: "The only reason I drew such difficult assignments was that the Department of State, probably wrongly, thought that I had some ability!" Laughter put an end to his interruption. Such people, I learned, react to humor the way the Wicked Witch of the West reacted to water: they simply cannot take it.

During that winter and spring, public concern over the danger of nuclear confrontation began to grow. I was appalled at the seeming insensitivity of the Reagan Administration to a perfectly understandable fear and to the desire on the part of the public that something, anything, be done to reduce the threat of global annihilation. At the same time, I did not believe that the anti-nuclear movement, based on simplistics and emotion and on symptoms rather than the underlying malady itself, would have any staying power, much less any lasting effect. I expressed these views in the March 1982 edition of *Reflections*, a local church magazine:

Too exclusive a focus on nuclear disarmament can give rise to the delusion that solving this one problem will get us out of danger on any long-term basis. The fundamental threat to us all lies in ourselves, our propensity to conflict, to violence, self-righteousness and self-delusion, to ego-tripping, to the avoidance of responsibility; in short, to all the flaws in our human nature that are conducive to war. Too exclusive a preoccupation with weaponry leaves less time for self-examination, for increasing our awareness of the world problems that give rise to its use, for pondering means for their resolution, and for developing a faith which might enable us to formulate fresh goals for our troubled planet.

However, the tide I was running against was strong. It took the form of the Nuclear Freeze Initiative, which advocated a bilateral freeze in the production, testing, and deployment of nuclear weapons, to be negotiated with the Soviet Union on a mutual and verifiable basis. Its adherents portrayed it as "only a first step," to reassure those aware of the complexities of arms control. Most successfully, it had translated an unarticulated concern about the nuclear-arms race into a specific proposal simple enough for the public to understand. As it turned out, the simplicity that made possible its initial appeal and support led over time to its loss of credibility. The Freeze movement could never define its own agenda. Its adherents never faced the reality that a freeze would take years to negotiate with the Soviets. How do you define a nuclear freeze? What is "nuclear" within that definition—only the weapon, or also its delivery system? After spending years in such negotiations, what specific steps did its adherents propose to take to reduce the number and lethalness of nuclear weapons? Or to verify that the conditions of the agreement were being met?

Moreover, a formula like the freeze, based on mutual deterrence, implied nuclear armaments of equal effectiveness on both sides. Since Soviet arsenals were relatively more modern than those of the United States, the United States would have to modernize its arsenals merely to maintain the rough equivalency on which the freeze was premised. That would require new weapons, something incompatible with a freeze as it was popularly understood. Moreover, the Freeze never addressed the question of whether modernization and new technology increased or decreased the threat of nuclear holocaust. New weapons might be more accurate, more localized in effect, and of lower destructive capacity. I even heard freeze proponents argue that, after the freeze was in effect, the United States should continue to rely on the weapons it had. Yet much of this is submarine-based, less accurate, and most effectively targeted on major urban centers. On moral as well as strategic grounds, this raised questions never really addressed by adherents of the freeze. Finally, the Freeze picked the wrong question for its primary focus. The ultimate issue is not the weapons, the hardware, but the underlying strategic assumptions that, under various sets of circumstances, might compel either side to use them.

As I soon discovered, none of these considerations would have had much effect on those who participated in a mass rally on Saturday, July 12, 1982, in New York's Central Park. On Sunday, many of the demonstrators came to the eleven o'clock service at the Cathedral, where I was scheduled to preach. As I climbed the pulpit stairs, vested in my red robe, an extreme peace activist stood up in the front pews and called out to the congregation: "Don't listen to this man. He's a wolf in sheep's clothing!" Mastering my anger as best I could, I began with a tribute to the "deep, deep concern for peace" that the rally had evidenced. I then went on:

While I have no doubt that an important message has been conveyed, one which no politician can ignore, there are problems raised by the session in the park—disturbing—just as the overall rally was encouraging. I think a great problem one always faces when one makes a statement, however eloquent, about the evils of a problem— and there is no more horrifying one than nuclear destruction—is that the statement itself may not have very much to do with the resolution of the problem . . . a statement that we don't like war, that we don't like nuclear weapons, doesn't get at the basic reasons why nations are arming. Similarly, I wonder sometimes about the oversimplification that we see coming out of rallies, such as the great rally yesterday in the park. How much we heard in the speeches yesterday that governments have appeared unsympathetic and unresponsive. We can therefore do without them. This is the cause of the people. This is in the hands of the people. The people will take peace into their own hands. Forgotten in this simplification is that it is, after all, governments that possess, and only they can dispose of, these weapons. The thought that the people can deal directly is extremely seductive. But I spent 444 days in the hands of a peace movement. The students called themselves a peace movement. I think all of you, although I was not, were witnesses to efforts to make peace in Iran when governments were *not* involved. You may recall [Secretary General] Kurt Waldheim on television, with distress manifest on his face, when there was no one with the accountability of government. Now, governments have their own problems. All too often they are locked into the past, and into past procedures. They need indeed the pressures of public opinion to make those set in their ways responsive and aware. But that does not mean that they are in any way dispensable.

And there is another delusion in this great delusion of simplification, that we can have action now. We have indeed waited thirty-five years. But in thirty-five years there have been twenty-one agreements. The nuclear problem is one of a complexity such as we have never faced, where technology and nationalism and ideology, all the great intractable problems, seem to meet. If we have not solved it in thirty-five years, we are not going to solve it *now*. That does not mean that we cannot solve it, but it means that enormous patience is called for.

There is another delusion that I heard coming out of the meetings yesterday, voiced on TV by Dick Gregory, who took off on all things intellectual. Now, he said, we have a concept that even Grandma can understand. No more experts, no more knowledge, no more experience. We have a simple idea that's going to solve everything and that's the "Freeze." And heaven help us, God *must* help us, if our only solutions to cancer, inflation, the problems of the City of New York, are to be reduced to one simple phrase, or to one simple concept. We are dealing with the most difficult of problems. What we have seen in this movement in the park is a return to "know-nothingism," which resists complexity when complex solutions are called for. This is a very, very great delusion . . .

By this time, a number of peace activists had gotten up and left the Cathedral, or after a barrage of shouting had been led out by the police. After the service, a peace activist shook his fist under my nose, shouting, "You're not a Christian." The time was fast coming, I realized, when I would find myself in opposition to Bishop Moore, who was becoming an enthusiastic advocate of the freeze. He had gone out of his way to befriend Louisa and me from the time of our arrival; he had been an enthusiastic participant in our conference on violence and religion and was most sympathetic to my difficulties with hecklers. Following the General Convention of the Episcopal Church, in which Louisa and I participated, he wrote to us on September 22, 1982:

I was so proud to have you both featured at General Convention. It does a lot for all of us to have you seen and heard as part of the Cathedral family. God bless you as always.

But then, on October 10, 1982, I preached a sermon at Trinity Church in Wilmington, Delaware, entitled "The Peace Movement and the Church." My remarks were prominently featured in the next day's *Wilmington News*. "Ex-hostage opposes nuclear-arms freeze" ran the headline. In the sermon itself, after paying tribute to the reach and vigor of the Freeze Initiative, I went on:

> I find the peace movement in some state of confusion, as if the movement had brought its adherents to a Red Sea of reality, whose waters will not easily part. And so they mill around, grasping at simplistic solutions, exploited by single-issue groups, with a dawning realization that rallying alone does not get anyone very far . . .

Someone sent Bishop Moore a copy of the article, and he sent me several admonitory memoranda. "If I were you, I'd stop seeming to make cracks at the Nuclear Freeze people. . . . I don't think it does your cause any good to sideswipe the movement as simplistic, because it includes some pretty sophisticated people in its ranks . . . especially your coming out against the Freeze, which is the official position of our National Church and our Diocesan Resolution . . . Characterizing the peace movement as 'people who mill around, grasping at simplistic solutions' won't do, as far as I'm concerned." And the Bishop went on: "The mass demonstration was carefully planned, and was an enormous success, with an international impact, and since that time there has been careful political action across the nation. If that's 'milling around,' then I don't know what that means."

As the Bishop, with his long experience, understood well, enthusiasm generated by a mass rally has to result in something fairly tangible fairly soon, or else it collapses. For that reason, time was a major factor in the Freeze movement. Often it took the form of fear deadlines in which the world was declared to be at five minutes to midnight. My major collision with the doomesday clock occurred in July 1984 in Chautauqua, where I was giving a series of afternoon lectures. One day the morning lecturer was Dr. Helen Caldicott, the anti-nuclear activist from Adelaide, who had declared that if Mr. Reagan was reelected that November the chances of nuclear war would be such that she would "go right back to Australia." Following my lecture, a peace activist still under Dr. Caldicott's spell berated me: "All right, you're telling us to develop sound judgment, to learn about complex international issues and all that. But what are we going to do between now and Election Day to prevent Armageddon?"

Well, Election Day 1984 has come and gone, and Mr. Reagan was returned to office by a landslide, and Dr. Caldicott is still in the United States, uttering a different lament. For the Freeze movement has collapsed. True, by stimulating millions of Americans to think more deeply about the perils of nuclear confrontation, it undoubtedly accomplished an important purpose. At the same time, it exposed Americans to the paradoxes of deterrence and the complexity of arms control, and in so doing, it educated them to the manifest inadequacies of the Freeze proposition itself. The Freeze thus prepared the way for its own demise. When the Reagan Administration advanced its Strategic Defense Initiative (Star Wars), a non-nuclear response which did not even depend on nuclear deterrence, Freeze advocates, whose thinking had been confined to the promulgation of their simple formula, had no effective reply.

On August 18, 1985, *The New York Times* printed a post-

mortem under the headline "Disarmament Groups Seek Rallying Point After Failure on Nuclear Freeze." A number of
anti-nuclear activists were interviewed, including Dr. Caldicott, who told the reporter: "There are more people educated
than ever before, and still we aren't winning." She said that
she would spend the next nine months thinking about possible strategies for the movement. As she does so, she might
reconsider her fear deadline and the other manipulations of
popular emotion that were so much a part of her tech-
nique. Three observations from my hostage experience might
be useful to her. The first has to do with "psychic numbing."
Dr. Caldicott has deplored a tendency on the part of the
American people to deny the reality of the nuclear threat.
She has described the "powerful defence mechanism of 'death
denial': we all survive by pretending we will never die." We
hostages, thinking that we faced execution, benefited greatly
from psychic numbing. So do we all. We would drive ourselves crazy if we kept thinking about our own death, or that
of our planet. What Dr. Caldicott failed to understand was that
her own constant harping on nuclear death brought on the
very numbing of which she complains. The nation became
numb to Dr. Caldicott and others like her, and to the serious
warnings these well-intentioned people sought to convey.

Second, as we hostages discovered with the release deadlines (out by Easter, out by Election Day, etc.), once the
deadline passes and nothing has happened, discouragement
is all the more profound. After the Freeze movement collapsed,
the moderates who had been stimulated to stuff envelopes
and carry signs drifted away. In the words of Randall Forsberg, one of the founders of Freeze, also quoted by *The New
York Times*, they were "tremendously disappointed and frustrated." In the face of such disillusionment, "we can't go out
and talk about the freeze and mobilize people again," Forsberg

concluded. "They are sitting home and doing nothing . . . The problem is that the public doesn't see a vehicle where they can place themselves in order to make a difference anymore."

In the end, we hostages learned to live on hope, the belief that our release was possible, and the expectation that everything necessary would be done to bring it about. Caldicott's promise that if she was elected President of the United States she would go to Moscow and settle the matter of nuclear confrontation in a few weeks was hardly reassuring. Caldicott and others like her left their hearers without hope, convinced that nothing could be done. But something can be done, and it is suggested in the words thrown back at me by Dr. Caldicott's disciple in Chautauqua: "to develop sound judgment, to learn about complex international issues, and all that."

Back in October 1982, my replies to Bishop Moore's admonitions were, so I thought, diplomatic, even irenic. For example, on October 28, I wrote:

Making clear from the outset that I saw problems as well as promise in the peace movement won me the confidence of a Wilmington congregation which, before my advent, had resisted the very idea of peace dialogue. Now, the rector informs me, he is in a position to invite to speak a wide spectrum of peace advocates, including some supporting the nuclear freeze.

As was not the case in prior peace manifestations, the church has within its grasp a major leadership role. That implies responsibility, and particularly that of ensuring that all voices are heard, all questions asked, and that no position is immune from continuing reexamination. Knowing that this is your hope as well, I am encouraged to continue in this difficult ministry. I need all the help I can get, and much appreciate yours.

But my efforts at objectivity and balance only perplexed the Bishop. "Here," he said to me, as we discussed my Wilmington sermon, "you say favorable things about the peace movement, but here"—and he jabbed the text with his index finger—"you criticize it." I was dealing, I realized, with a mind-set that was very different from mine. Paul Moore was of the 1960s, one of those clergy who were faced with an explosion of social and political issues of profound moral dimension which little in their seminary or parish experience had prepared them to address. This notwithstanding, in they plunged, innovatively, courageously, and, given the special circumstances of the 1960s, often successfully. Paul Moore in his pioneering inner-city mission in Jersey City from 1949 to 1957, for example, provided a model for important new ministries in the Episcopal Church.

Yet many of the issues they faced—racial segregation, for instance—either were morally unambiguous or, as in the case of Vietnam, could be made to appear as simple matters of principle susceptible of very simple and often negative solutions: Abolish (Jim Crow). Get out of (Vietnam). In few of these issues was their self-confidence put to the test of confronting moral ambiguity, or factual complexity, or the possibility that someone coming at the same problem from a very different direction might also be "right." In my Wilmington sermon, I tried to address the problem:

Another pitfall is a tendency to oversimplify. Declarations that dangers exist, descriptions, however eloquent, of horrors such as the threat of nuclear destruction, do not of themselves point to solutions of problems which are necessarily complex. Churches are not always sufficiently aware of their lack of knowledge and experience in these areas. They forget that God does not always reward faith with perfect understanding. Parallel with this is the absence of accountability for problems and their solutions. To those not responsible for their solutions, political problems often seem easier to resolve than they really are.

In his admonition of October 22, the Bishop, perhaps without realizing it, made my point for me:

> The idea, however, that we should stop manufacturing weapons as soon as possible is a sound one—even though working out that principle would take complicated diplomatic maneuvers.

What would make the principle "sound" was indeed whether or not it was susceptible of "complicated diplomatic maneuvers." In his last admonition, dated November 10, which—a bit ominously, I thought—had "Bishop of New York" typed under his name, he informed me that he found my nuclear unbelief "a little upsetting, since many of your close colleagues are working as hard as they can for the Freeze." In fact, he felt "betrayed," so Dean Morton explained to me, and the Bishop, red-faced with anger, would pass me in the corridor of Cathedral House with the barest of acknowledgments.

My relationship with the higher clergy was further complicated by the failure of the capital campaign. On the basis of donations which never materialized, financial commitments had been piled one on top of another, including, as one example, a Columbia MBA hired at a very high salary as the marketing manager. By December 1982, the Cathedral was in serious financial straits, and the future of the Peace Institute was in jeopardy.

After all the publicity attendant on bringing a hostage couple on board, and given the growing visibility and reputation of the Peace Institute, I seriously wondered how the Cathedral could pull the rug out from under me so soon after my recruitment. On December 15, 1982, the Bishop and I had a most cordial conversation in which it was agreed that, so long as its personnel costs and office expenses from then on could be met from sources other than the Cathedral budget, the Peace Institute would be welcome to stay where it was. I summarized our understanding in a letter of December 28 to the Bishop, and from various outside sources I raised funds sufficient to keep the Peace Institute in business at least until May 1983. On January 17, 1983, I so advised the Bishop in writing. On January 19, however, the Executive Committee of the Trustees, without informing me, voted to "remove" Marie Moser and myself "from the Cathedral budget." And they reallocated, for past expenses, the modest funding I had just raised to continue the Peace Institute. Then, on March 4, Marie Moser and I were fired retroactively, effective February 1, with the amount of the two biweekly paychecks already paid to us offset against the severance that was due us. I went all over the Cathedral Close informing everyone I met that I planned to bring proceedings before the New York State Labor Board. Marie Moser's letter of remonstrance to the Bishop left the trustees with little to say. Not long after, my conditions, including severance for my assistant, were complied with in full.

In April and May 1983, I closed down the Peace Institute. My bizarre misadventures at the Cathedral, for which I had been quite unprepared, had triggered the overdue psychic reaction to captivity of which Esther Roberts, back at the Department, had warned me. Yet, while they set back my recovery from my Iranian experience quite measurably, they deepened my faith. More especially, they forced me to consider a question that had puzzled me from my early days at the Cathedral: What moved this Bishop, so outspoken in his support of liberal causes and so conscious of his liberal image, and so often kindly, so devoted to the cause of peace, to behave in such a manner? For this has implications that go well beyond his outlook and his ecclesiastical position.

I finally concluded that the mind-set of the 1960s clergy, which tended to direct their attention to issues of this world, has not in any fundamental way diminished their need for religious certainty. These clergy merely seek the equivalent of religious certainty in the causes they advocate. By this transference they become true believers who insist that the Freeze is the only approach, who claim far too much for it, who regard any questioning as heresy and, particularly from colleagues, as betrayal. Thus, chiding me for my skepticism about the Freeze, another senior church official reminded me sharply that I was attacking people's beliefs. Commenting on this confusion, a senior Lutheran official wrote to me deploring the "intolerance that seems to beset the Christian community generally today on the question of nuclear deterrence. Indeed, Christians seem to be on the verge of theological violence." As I stated on a television program later broadcast by New York's Trinity Church: "I've felt in some groups that I would have a much easier time denying the Resurrection than I would have questioning the Nuclear Freeze."

Such credal politics are often aggravated by another tendency, which I had addressed in my Wilmington sermon:

And most serious of all, there sometimes surfaces in churches an arrogance, an intolerance, a smug self-righteousness. The tendency that produced the Crusades, the feeling that those who oppose us are wrong, that they're not *our* enemies but *God's*, is hidden away in most of us who believe. The Moral Majority is an exaggerated example of this. Iran today is another. But we all suffer from it. And the peace movement is certainly not immune. On the contrary.

I might have added words such as "absolutism," "obscurantism," "know-nothingism," "dogmatism," and "authoritarianism," not to mention "fanaticism." For I was talking about the Ayatollah, who, as I think of him, is far more than one Iranian cleric. He is that bundle of negative feelings within all of us that prevent us from listening to one another. Through him, we ascribe our political views to the Almighty and assert them as if they were His revelation. The Ayatollah encourages us to believe that we can trample roughshod on the common garden decencies that make life tolerable for others. And he prevents us in a variety of ways from growing up internationally as well as personally.

In April and May 1983, I received two honorary doctorates, one from the University of Pittsburgh, the other from Middlebury College. The accompanying citations referred to the contribution to the understanding of peace that I had made through the Cathedral Peace Institute. I moved to the Myrin Institute in May 1983, where, under the name of the Council for International Understanding, the work continues.

9 / DELIVERING
THE MESSAGE

CONTRARY TO EXPECTATIONS, my hostage visibility did not quickly wither and die. Anniversaries of the takeover, the rescue attempt, and our release have provided opportunity for TV networks hungry for events, and I soon became one of the two or three former hostages called upon to appear. The resurgence in 1985 of terrorist activity brought more camera crews to my office in search of comment. The Iranian hostage experience itself, etched into the consciousness of the American public by television, demanded to be told and told again. I drew on its drama not simply to tell stories but to illustrate the point I wanted made about foreign affairs. My audiences since February 1981 ranged from the Union Theological Seminary in New York City to the Chautauqua Institution, to the Episcopal Cathedral in Spokane; from St. Paul's, a small black college in southern Virginia, to the Kennedy School of Government at Harvard University; from an IBM awards ceremony in Miami Beach to the isle of Iona in Scotland's Inner Hebrides.

My academic background being strictly Ivy League and conventional, I was increasingly impressed with the innovation I found in smaller, less well known institutions, particularly in community colleges. I also began to understand the clergy better than I had before. After quiet evenings in rectories and parsonages listening to them talk about their jobs, I recognized how extraordinarily difficult their task is, and how well so many are coping. In many ways, they are like Foreign Service officers, well educated, a little apart from the rest of society in their motivations, and not well understood or sufficiently appreciated.

For all my public-speaking experience, I found that I still had a great deal to learn. Particularly among church groups, my approach in that initial period was entirely too confrontational. Intent upon the message that I was trying to convey, and encouraged by positive responses from most who came to hear me, I would forget that some in the audience might approach these same problems from a different perspective. If I hoped to engage in worthwhile dialogue, possibly to change their views, I would have to think as well as to say "we" instead of "you."

Not everybody welcomed my efforts. Almost predictably, the Reverend William Sloane Coffin in September 1983 wrote a letter to the Forum for Corporate Responsibility in New York, protesting a lecture, "Nuclear Disarmament—A Pragmatic View," that I was shortly to deliver. As a seasoned church official explained this kind of resistance, it was because I was a moderate. Extreme peace activists were used to handling their fellow extremists on the right. They shared the same single-issue, black-and-white approach. But I was in the center, with an approach that tried to take the ambiguities and anomalies of life and statecraft into account. I had the credibility given me by my hostage experience; the fact that I had served in the Foreign Service could be held against me and was. In any event, I was threatening and difficult to reply to.

Among moderates, my message was more readily accepted. As the rector of a church in a New York suburb wrote to me after I had addressed its adult study forum: "One man's comment symbolized the response of many. He said to me: 'I came here expecting to be made furious by these talks. But instead I find that I have been made to do some serious thinking in channels I hadn't expected.' If," the rector concluded, "we could always achieve that, we'd be in clover." I was delighted, also, to find younger audiences, of school and college age, responsive to my ideas.

In February 1985, I returned to the Department of State to speak to the Secretary's Open Forum on "The Foreign Service and the Peace Movement." The Department then asked me to repeat the same lecture at four Embassies abroad. Following my retirement, I had stayed away from the Department and from Washington itself. I was reluctant to be perceived as one of the many retired officers who somehow cannot break away. Further, my leaving the Foreign Service had not fully resolved my ambivalence toward it. But my welcome was warm, even moving, including lunch with some of my former subordinates, who were doing very well indeed. In Europe, I was invited to attend staff meetings, where I felt once again the extraordinary collegiality around the table that is one of the joys of the career.

The peace movement, I told my Foreign Service audiences, was a manifestation of populism, which is in part a reaction against professionalism. It flourishes when professionals are thought not to be doing their jobs properly, or not delivering what they are paid for. Peace activists, and many Americans who subscribed to the Nuclear Freeze, no longer felt secure. They were fearful and deeply worried. Peace activists argue that "it is experts who have gotten us all into this mess"— nuclear confrontation or whatever. "Let's give peace back to the people . . . we want peace now." The Nuclear Freeze was a vote not merely by hard-core peace activists. It included moderates, people of balance who had lost confidence in the way our foreign relations were being managed and in those charged with their management. I reviewed some of the lessons that should have been learned from the Tehran takeover and were not. In conclusion, I pointed out that extremists on the right, as well as those on the peace side, were commanding more attention than their simplistic thinking deserved. The development of popular support for a sound and balanced foreign policy depends in part on the Foreign Service's example, which in turn will require more innovative professionalism.

Almost from the beginning, I addressed the problem of foreign students and their response to their American experience. Reminding my audience that some of my captors had been students in the United States, I noted, in a lecture at Princeton University in November 1984:

We have in the foreign student community in this country something that could be a terrible time bomb or a tremendous source of international understanding—both in what they come to know about us and in what American students learn from them. We are training a generation not only of foreign leaders but of American leaders, and it is terribly important therefore that our foreign students not be isolated, that they mix, form a part of the community of the universities where they are studying, for their sake, but even more for our own.

But the principal burden of my lectures and remarks around the country was that peace activism was doomed to ineffectiveness so long as it focused on single issues external to ourselves, rather than where the real battle had to be fought, within ourselves. Our daily lives, and our relations with one another,

I argued, are a microcosm for peace-making activity on a larger scale. In a commencement address at the University of Pittsburgh, on April 24, 1983, I asked:

Now, what does domestic peace-making have to do with international peace-making, with how we're going to prevent a war? All right, so I'm a peace-maker, so I try to understand where the other person is coming from, I try not to confront him. I try to find common ground. What's that to do with the Soviets? What's that got to do with not being blown up? I would say this, that the peace-making you do at every level of human transaction is what's going to heal our country. It's what's going to make us work together as a nation, an integrated nation, a country that doesn't have to resort to a lot of macho, to a lot of hysterics, to a lot of decibels, to a lot of scare psychology. It's going to be a country that's internally strong, in just the way a lot of very big strong men can be very gentle men, because nobody has ever dared to push them around. That is the kind of country that is a source of world peace.

Self-understanding as a basis for effective citizenship had to focus, I told my audiences, on two problems. The first is the moral confusion with which we view foreign affairs, one that stems from reluctance to face squarely the way we make decisions in our own lives. The second problem is found in our cultural obstacles to the understanding of other peoples. My basic concern, however, was to suggest to my audiences that they relate "abroad" to the experience of their own lives.

Once, for example, when I found myself facing an early-morning history class at a secondary school, it was instantly clear that my first task was to wake the students up. Setting aside my notes, I asked the eleventh-graders to take a piece of paper and draw a line down the middle. I then asked them to list on one side all the words or phrases that were called to mind by the word "Arab." The reader can imagine what emerged—volatile, fanatical, dirty, ignorant, undemocratic, inefficient, disorganized, insensitive to the poor. I then asked them to list words they associated with "American." Once again, the response was predictable—all the middle-class virtues, including a high standard of hygiene. Americans were steadfast, efficient, prudent, democratic, balanced, orderly, and all the rest. I then went down the "Arab" list, reminding them of filthy New York subway stations; abrupt changes in our foreign policy; of the fanaticism of those who bomb abortion clinics; the inefficiency involved in the hostage rescue attempt; and so forth. Going down the "American" list, I noted, by contrast with Americans, how deliberate and conservative the Saudis are, particularly in reaching important decisions; how Islam is inherently democratic in concept; how almsgiving and ritual ablutions before prayer are part of Islamic observance. I hope that, as well as seeing how stereotypes cut both ways, my students learned something about the Middle East and about their own attitudes.

Secondary-school and college students were particularly amused when I told them how the Imam Khomeini had ordered Western-style toilets ripped out of a major Iranian resort hotel and replaced them with what our Marines called "bombsights"—places for your feet, and a hole. This was a phase of the revolutionary effort to expunge Western values and replace them with traditional Islamic or Iranian values. The toilet, after all, is more than a physical convenience. How you use it becomes fundamental to your cultural identity.

My proudest distinction as a private first class in the U.S. Army, I would go on, was as latrine orderly. Whenever a colonel's inspection was due, PFC Kennedy would be detailed to clean the washrooms. He could get the scum off the shower stalls in no time flat . . . When in December 1979 we hostages were moved to the basement of the Chancery, the two washrooms, now for common use, showed the result of two months of student use. They were revolting. I demanded a mop and a bucket and set to work. After a few hours, "Men" was ready. The next day, I did "Women." And so forth.

My biggest problem, I pointed out to my classes, was that Iranians do not use toilet paper. Instead, they use water, which their floor-level latrines are equipped to collect. When they used American-style facilities, the water, once it had accomplished its salubrious purpose, would end up on the floor, where I had to mop it up. The hardest part, I would note, was cleaning the footprints off the toilet seats. By this time, the girls in the class particularly were giggling and exchanging glances. But, I would conclude, is there any reason to suppose that one way to go to the bathroom is necessarily better than another? From the point of view of avoiding direct contact with porcelain, the Muslim way is far more hygienic. It is only when you mix cultural assumptions that problems arise.

To the Bar Association of San Antonio, I made the same point, in a different way. Referring to my law-school studies, which had compared the inheritance laws of Massachusetts and Islamic law, I observed that, in fulfilling its own ethical norms, the Islamic system of inheritance was far more successful than Anglo-American law. Essentially, Anglo-American law protects the right of testators to do what they want with their wealth, subject only to the law's insistence that there be some protection for spouses. In the Islamic system, what the testator may dispose of freely is strictly limited; provision must be made not only for children but also for parents. The one system is essentially a statement of one's rights; the other, of one's duties. Which is superior or more civilized?

In October 1984, I directed a weekend retreat for lay people in a monastery overlooking the Hudson River. It was my first experience of monastic life; calling back a loud, clear "Thanks be to God!" when one of the brothers banged on my door to wake me at 5:30 in the morning was not how I usually addressed my alarm clock. I was not yet aware of how the monastery's spiritual atmosphere tended to heighten the impact of what was presented. The theme of the retreat was "peace within, peace in the world." The participants, who, not unnaturally, had come expecting to discuss "peace" and to be commended for their peaceable attitudes, were not prepared for what I was about to do. In Scripture we read: "I bring not peace but a sword." I was bringing the sword of self-examination that must precede inner growth and the achievement of inner peace. In the morning session, I discussed the moral confusion in all of us which distorts our understanding of foreign affairs. In the afternoon, I took up cultural barriers to the same understanding. By the end of the afternoon, I found that the group had been turned off. Some, including one seminarian, avoided meeting my eyes as we left for supper. "We were hoping for something more spiritual," another said to me. "There is a lot of anger in them," one of the monks suggested. "Perhaps you are laying on them more than they are ready to handle."

Fortunately, we entered the period called the Great Silence. Because no one was allowed to speak, I could not feel badly at supper if no retreatant spoke to me. After supper, we gathered in a circle in the library, and I began to relate some of my experiences as a hostage, beginning with my feelings at the time when I thought I was going to be executed. Then I asked the participants to contribute some fundamental experiences of their own which had altered their thinking and their lives. As they opened up, they began to refer to things I had said in the course of the day. Clearly, they had taken in more than I had dared hope, or they to admit. Equally clearly, it was necessary for the material I had presented to be related to their personal experiences. Only then could they accept and draw on it for use in their lives. At the close of the retreat, several volunteered that they had been through a growth experience in which their inchoate feelings about peace were tried in ways that would help them to achieve both self-understanding and inner peace, which they recognized as the first step in becoming effective citizens.

10 / MORAL
CONFUSION

HAROLD H. SAUNDERS, Assistant Secretary of State for Near Eastern and South Asian Affairs during the Iranian hostage crisis,
has described how

> . . . throughout this period, there was a proliferation
> of private groups and individuals who felt that their
> going to Tehran in an unofficial capacity could provide
> an American sounding-board for Iran's expression of
> grievances against the U.S. . . . The hostages themselves,
> in some cases, were bitter that the efforts of some indi-
> viduals to appear sympathetic to Iranian militants and
> critical of the United States actually made their position
> as American officials even more difficult.

Saunders was referring, among others, to the Easter clergy.
None of these well-intentioned gestures helped. Our captivity
was destined to last as long as it helped to maintain revolutionary fervor, and no confession of America's sinful ways
could have made it worth our captors' while to release us. The
delusion that an apologetic stance is the key to successful

negotations dies hard among peace activists. One of them used to argue that we should begin the next round of arms-control negotiations by apologizing. I thought back to the very successful lend-lease negotiations with the Soviets in which I had taken part. Had we begun with an apology—accepting, for example, their contention that it was the Soviet Union which had carried the burden of the war against the Nazis, and so they should pay nothing—the negotiations would have failed. Among other reasons, our Soviet counterparts would not have considered us serious people. There is a major difference between listening to the message that the other side is sending and abjectly accepting their contention that "it's all America's fault."

Moreover, because they failed to think through the probable consequences of what they said and did, the Easter clergy only added to our difficulties. By accepting the students' allegation that the Embassy was a nest of spies (whether it was or not), they thought they would facilitate relations with our captors and thus improve the chances of our release. But their statements might well have been used against us in a revolutionary court. "Hawks" as much as "doves" have problems seeing beyond their intentions to probable consequences. Those who advocated avenging America's national humiliation by bombing Iran failed to consider not only the moral implications of such an assault but also its consequences—certain death for us and many others, and the escalation of hostilities, including possible Soviet military intervention. As one of my cellmates replied to another one who advocated military reprisal: "We're fifty-two guys, one busload, one platoon—we're not worth a war."

With hawks and doves, we see an absence of mature judgment, sometimes defined as the inability to cope with ambiguity; mature people can hold opposites in balance, and recognize that nothing is black or white, in ordinary life or in foreign affairs. The mature can weigh their ideals against the necessity to survive. This is perhaps best illustrated by the seemingly contradictory ways in which we define peace. There is peace in the ideal sense, which Christians often refer to as "the peace that passeth all understanding." To Jews *shalom* means the same. No one can define *shalom* precisely, yet many of us have caught glimpses of it and have an intimation of what it signifies. I did, as I faced the possibility of execution. Peace in this sense is self-fulfillment, a right relationship with ourselves, our families, our fellow human beings, and our Creator. Mankind has a powerful longing for this goal, but the peace it envisages is one that the world cannot give.

At peace meetings, one hears quoted the passage from Micah and Isaiah about beating swords into ploughshares, and nation not lifting up sword against nation. For Jews, the passage describes the coming of the Messiah. In its Christian interpretation, it means the coming of Christ's Kingdom. Admittedly, for the convinced Christian pacifist, the Kingdom has already come, and convinced pacifists are governed by its laws. But in the Jewish tradition and in the Christian mainstream this passage describes the millennium. There is therefore no guarantee in Scripture that the human race will until then be free of the flaws in its nature. Until we are free, we will always have to come to terms with an unjust, cruel, and often dangerous world.

Nations, like individuals, act in fear and self-interest, which often leads to violence and war. People are greedy; they are improvident; they seek fulfillment at the expense of others. To counter what persons and nations might do to each other to attain self-fulfillment is to enforce justice. And enforcing justice makes possible another kind of peace, sometimes referred to by the Latin word *pax*. This is the peace of enforcement, of deterrence and coercion, swords rather than ploughshares.

Quite properly, we call a sheriff a peace officer, even though he carries a gun to enforce his authority. The latent threat of a jail sentence is the ultimate tax collector; an armed National Guard has helped to enforce civil rights.

In the Tehran hostage situation, the availability and potential use of armed force prevented a crisis from escalating into armed conflict. In commenting on the Carter Administration's wise decision not to attack Iran because of the takeover of the Embassy, former Deputy Secretary of State Warren Christopher qualified his remarks:

> For there is some evidence that one precisely targeted, very explicit military threat did have some effect on the behavior of the Iranians. In the first days after the hostages were taken, their captors announced that they were about to be tried as spies and executed. The White House publicly suggested that any such trials would bring a U.S. military response. Then, on November 23, the President followed up with a private message to Iran which left no doubt that if the hostages were harmed there would be military retribution.

Although we did not know of Carter's threat, Hossein Sheikholeslam, during our basement conversation in February 1980, warned us that if the United States did not meet the students' terms, they would be forced to turn us over to the revolutionary courts. Our Marines, mere guards, would undoubtedly be let off, he indicated, but the rest of us would face trial, and some of us would be executed. Mailman had confirmed that among the students one group, a minority, wanted us executed. President Carter's threat of retaliation undoubtedly strengthened the hand of those who wanted us kept alive. In communicating that threat, Carter helped not only to save our lives but also to avoid the consequences of military intervention.

In the middle of the TWA hostage crisis, when American popular feeling was understandably running high, I wrote an article for the *Miami Herald* in which, after citing the argument that unless we retaliate, we will see future crises, I went on:

> It might help to decide what kind of sanctions we are talking about. There are two kinds of threats of retaliation, the "if" or deterrent kind, and the "unless" or action-forcing kind. Very rightly, President Carter threatened prompt military retaliation if our captors executed us, or brought us to trial . . . President Reagan seems to have been talking about the action-forcing kind. On this threat, unless hostages are released, something awful will happen to their captors. Exponents of this theory forget that just as the United States refuses to negotiate "at the point of a gun," so likewise the hostage-holder, Nabih Berri, or whoever might play the key role in similar future hostage crises, cannot be seen by his extremist peers to be knuckling under. So he rejects the threat.
>
> The President making the threat, Reagan or whoever, is left with an uncomfortable choice. If he does not follow through, he will look foolish. If he does follow through and the threat is not credible (i.e., bombing the Beirut airport), he will look even more foolish. If his sanctions are serious ones—for example, bombing Baalbek, the Shiite center in eastern Lebanon, with the loss of innocent lives—he can generate reactions that can turn against Americans in the future.
>
> Of course, we should retaliate against the two original hijackers who murdered a Navy diver if we can identify and locate them.

Like Warren Christopher in his discussion of Carter's retaliatory threat, and as I felt strongly after the murder by terrorists of Leon Klinghoffer in October 1985, I was advocating the measured and discriminatory use of force, proportionate to the injury suffered, and most likely to achieve the objective sought. Force is neither rejected nor relied on to the exclusion of other means of resolving international disputes. Many peace activists, however, reject its use altogether, finding justification for their position in the model of Gandhi's non-violent resistance to British rule. In imitation of Gandhi, such resisters go through civil-disobedience training, in which they are taught, among other things, how to lie down preparatory to being picked up and carted off by the police, who in turn receive special training on how to pick up and cart off peace activists. Without the benefit of CD training, and facing the prospect of the ultimate violence, we hostages engaged in non-violent resistance, of which the episode of Mailman and the photographs for my wall is an example. Because he wanted our respect, he was willing to make a peace offering. Also, because many of the student guards were troubled by the ethical implications of what they were doing, there developed limits on their behavior which, reinforced by Mr. Carter's threat, were not often overstepped.

Gandhi was, I believe, a special case. The success of his kind of non-violent resistance depends not only on the sincerity and skill of the resister but also on the moral character of the oppressor. To a large extent, non-violent resistance succeeded in India because the British Raj was by and large restrained, consisting mostly of decent (if often prejudiced) people who were not without lurking doubts about the permanence, if not the legitimacy, of their role. Had Gandhi been up against the Nazis or the Soviets, the story would have been very different. Peace activists who reject force in and of itself, who consider non-violent resistance a substitute for the armed defense of Europe against the Soviets, have read the wrong lessons in history. We hostages survived in part through non-violent resistance and related survival techniques, but also thanks to the combination of negotiating flexibility and potential for armed intervention deployed by the Carter Administration. Military force, properly used, can save lives and preserve peace and justice.

By what criteria, then, do we judge the rightness of an act of military intervention, or any other act of state in the international arena? We have already distinguished two definitions of peace, *shalom* and *pax*. Similarly, we must be precise about the nature of the morality we are discussing. Related to the apocalyptic vision of peace is the morality of the challenge to perfection, the uncompromising law of love found in the Sermon on the Mount. Persons, institutions, even nations sometimes respond to this challenge. They can act with extraordinary decency—but only on occasion. They cannot be counted on to do so consistently. This was brought home to me at a staff meeting at Embassy Santiago, when we were discussing a demarche to our hosts, the Chilean government, on human-rights abuses. Regarding such an action on our part as an unwarranted intervention in their domestic affairs, the Pinochet regime directed its anger against Ambassador David Popper. Yet, knowing full well that the proposed demarche would be costly to him in terms of his personal acceptability and effectiveness, Popper said, smiling gently, "I don't pretend to be an expert on Christianity, but this, I think, is what the Christian faith would tell us to do." Part of what made this statement remarkable was that Popper is Jewish. It stuck in my mind, however, because nations and their representatives abroad do not usually formulate decisions, or justify them, in such terms. The world, as it is, does not often permit it.

The peace which has to be enforced, which equates with justice, requires another kind of morality, and that calls for hard choices and possibly distasteful actions. The two moralities are distinct; at the same time, they interpenetrate. The

visionary peace embodying the law of love provides a re-
deeming element in the enforcement of justice and the morality of hard choice, but enforcement of justice, besides keeping
us alive in a less than perfect world, enables us to defend the
peace. Reinhold Niebuhr put this very well when he said that
justice without love ceases to be justice, becoming no more
than balance of power; and love without justice ceases to be
love, degenerating into mere sentimentality.

At the bottom of much popular dissatisfaction with present
American foreign policy is the sense that it lacks positive
goals for a better world, that it is merely an exercise in balance of power. As a counterpart, this sentimental side of the
Niebuhr equation has surfaced at many peace meetings I have
attended, not infrequently in churches. To me, this is surpris-
ing. It is, after all, heresy for Christians to deny the validity
of the Old Testament, which the New Testament complements
but does not displace. The Old Testament, the story of the
Fall of Man, documents some of the things we may have to do
in this world in order to survive and to secure justice.

Often, in church groups, I find myself responding to criti-
cisms of policies such as United States government support
of counterrevolutionaries, or contras, or indeed any use of
United States power. I often note that in the management of
their own affairs, most notably in their elections, churches, like
civil governments, must act on the morality of hard choice.
Churches use the very elements of fear and self-interest on
which political strategy depends. With their politics no cleaner
than anyone else's, they will do the distasteful thing if it brings
about the desired result. Yet they often criticize government
for acting on the basis of the same morality of hard choice. Alternatively, they criticize government for not assuming that
standard of perfection to which they do not feel confined. This
brings us to the vexing problem of consequential ethics. Let
me note that, with its traditions of survival, the Jewish faith

is particularly attuned to consequential ethics. Rabbinical tradition reminds us that the end instructs us about a matter. Even the Ten Commandments say nothing about intent. Many Christians, however, mindful of the call to perfection and the law of love as they interpret it, find consequential ethics more than a little disturbing. Good intentions are so much easier!

It is not a matter of choosing between right intentions and their consequences. We are stuck with both. The problem we face is how to keep them in balance. An imbalance between concern for right intention and regard for consequences indicates unsound judgment. It does not matter whether we are talking about hawks or doves. The revulsion of extreme hawks toward world communism and the revulsion of extreme peace activists toward nuclear weapons are similar in one respect. Both, in their rectitude, demand unilateral action by the United States. If the solution advocated by the one is a preemptive nuclear strike, the other's is the total divestiture of nuclear weapons.

Were it beyond question that possession of weapons leads to their use, the peace activist would have a valid argument. But what if possession serves to dissuade others from using weapons? So long as this is a reasonable probability, we have no right not to maintain nuclear arsenals, not to modernize them in ways likely to enhance deterrence. Whatever the assumptions about the effectiveness of deterrence, revulsion for such weapons, which we all share, cannot by itself determine the issue. On the other hand, when regard for consequences outweighs concern for right intentions, we encounter the same problem. It does not matter whether we are talking about hawks or doves. The hawk who sees the Soviet Union primarily as a military threat to the survival of the United States, to be attacked preemptively before it can attack us, is using consequential reasoning to excess—never mind the moral cost. The same excess of consequentiality is found in the argument often voiced by peace activists that no values are worth preserving at the risk of a nuclear war, since, as one commentator put it, nuclear war would at best result in a republic of insects and grass. If everyone is dead, of what use are values?

Both the extreme hawks, with the preemptive strike, and the extreme doves, with their preemptive capitulation, are practicing survivalist ethics, which are consequential ethics gone amok. They set at naught not merely the values for which I, for one, was willing to die—among them, freedom and respect for the integrity of the human personality—but the existence of any values at all. As the philosopher Sidney Hook said: when a person makes survival the highest objective, he has declared that there is nothing he will not betray. In a world of collapsing moral values, where only the strong survive—at the expense of the weak—anarchy coupled with terror kills more than people. It renders life itself intolerable. In this connection, American physicians, who as a group have not played much of a role in politics or world affairs, in the days of the Nuclear Freeze suddenly became very active on the issue of nuclear war and made an important contribution. Some, however, have evinced an ethic that is purely consequential, purely survivalist, the result of a lifelong professional commitment to the preservation of human life. But those who cope with "vegetables" among the elderly have cruel reminders that there is perhaps more to human life than vital signs. No group is more aware of this than doctors.

We next come to a third aspect of mature judgment in life and in foreign affairs—the recognition that we are all flawed. Explanations for the darker side of human nature are many. Christians may recall St. Paul, who in Romans 7 burst out: "For what I will to do, that I do not practice; but what I hate, that I do." Extremists who cannot keep intention and consequences in balance will not admit that we are flawed, that none of us has a monopoly on righteousness, that Original Sin is not unevenly divided. For the extreme political right, Original Sin resides exclusively with the Soviets. They are the Devil Incarnate, whereas America, with her terrible swift sword, is God's avenging angel. Because we as a nation can do no wrong, the Soviets must be absolutely wrong. In any event, since you do not compromise with the Devil, America's positions must be non-negotiable. That, indeed, was the ideological mind-set of the Reagan Administration when it came to office; it was soon modified by experience.

On the other side of the political spectrum, among extreme peace activists and some of our visitors in Iran, Original Sin resides exclusively with the government of the United States, or with the American people. At peace meetings I have attended, the atmosphere of guilt and self-reproach—that "it's all our fault"—is so thick as to be overpowering. Too easily, extreme peace people can allow their guilt to run wild, leading to the conclusion that since we are guilty, the Soviets must be guiltless. We then hear about the United States and Central America, but rarely about the Soviet Union and Central Asia. Admittedly, the United States government has made mistakes in its foreign relations. It has also done things of which we all may be proud. On balance, however, the perception of extreme activists that our foreign policy is altogether wrong is a denial of basic human experience—our policies, like ourselves, are not altogether good, nor are they altogether bad. Yet many peace activists hold that, because of our imperfections, we have forfeited the right to advance our own priorities from strength and with flexibility in the negotiating process. Not enough is said about imperfections and consequent forfeitures on the part of the Soviets.

Whether expressed as self-righteousness or as self-hatred, whether by hawk or by dove, the moral absolutism that these positions represent is the antithesis of maturity. A responsible approach to foreign affairs begins with the recognition that we are all fallible. If none of us is altogether right or wrong, then there must be some right on the other side, some interests we should respect, just as we expect others to respect ours. That is where negotiation begins.

Recognition and acceptance of our common fallibility does not mean that we have to deny that our enemies are indeed enemies. The Christian mandate to love your enemies does not mean that we have to like them or approve of what they have done to us or take the blame for their misdeeds upon ourselves. There is no way that our captors in Iran can escape the full burden of responsibility for all that happened to the hostages. Or Arab terrorists for crimes committed.

Yet even we hostages recognized that it was not that simple, either. A month before our release, as we began to realize that the end of our captivity was in sight and to think back on what it all meant, a Marine roommate suddenly asked: "Say, suppose we were guards and they were the hostages—would we have treated them as well as they treated us?" Since the conditions of our imprisonment had not been good, he was not complimenting their behavior. What he recognized was that we were probably not inherently any better than they. Potentially, we were as capable as anyone else of the greatest wrongs.

Admitting that we share a common fallibility enables us to recognize that we also share a common responsibility. It was not just the Department of State that "betrayed" us in Iran; I, too, was involved. As Louisa used to remind her fellow hostage wives: "Look, like it or not, it's the only State Department we've got." And, like it or not, it's the only world we've got, including Iranians and Arabs. With that recognition, we learn not to seek scapegoats, not to point the finger of blame. And as we share responsibility, we learn to reach out to one another. We learn to understand how and why others perceive the world differently than we do, how to accommodate those differences and how to identify common interests and common goals. As a responsible people, we learn to put the problem on one side of the table and ourselves on the other, the better to work toward common solutions.

Finally, mature judgment can be achieved, whether addressing an international issue or a personal problem, if we understand the process by which we reach difficult decisions. The first essential is to ask ourselves: What interests are involved? Most issues involve a multiple of interests, often in conflict, as well as an admixture of motives. For instance, support for the democratic process in Third World countries is in the American interest. Is it because we believe it to be good; because we traditionally stand for democratic values and a failure to support them would diminish our reputation abroad; because we recognize that tyranny leads, over time, to revolution and anarchy and hence undermines the stable world we seek? But support for the democratic process cannot be treated in isolation from our many other interests, including concern for our nation's survival. We need to look at various courses of action and ask whether each is likely to do what its proponents claim it will do, whether it is consistent with other courses of action, and whether we have foreseen all probable consequences. Only after this kind of sorting out has taken place can we get to the key question: Is what we want and the way we plan to achieve it morally acceptable?

Some readers may question this reasoning, arguing that we must ask the moral question at every stage, or that putting it last means we consider it least. Neither, I believe, is correct. Indeed, much of the moral confusion that so diminishes the effectiveness of peace activism arises in part because such questions are asked in reverse order. Asking the moral question first usually indicates an imbalance between intentions and possible consequences. More dangerously, if we proclaim our moral concern before we acknowledge our interests, then we not only deceive ourselves as to our real motives but we bewilder others. President Carter's human-rights policies, for example, gave others the opportunity to call us hypocrites. Indeed, our frequent self-deception as to our real motives is a major reproach leveled by foreigners. In their approach to the problem of Nicaragua, for example, neither hawks nor doves address the question of what our real interests are. If we have real interests to defend in Central America, then offering limited support to counterrevolutionaries is not enough. On the grounds of self-defense, we should intervene. On the other hand, if we have no real interests in the area, even limited support is far too much.

Thus, in international relations as in our own lives, we must begin by asking ourselves what our real interests are. What do we really want? We need to assess and then rank those interests, and choose between or reconcile divergent courses of action and their possible consequences. Then we must ask the all-important question: Have we any right to demand this or that for ourselves, or any right not to perform this or that duty, however inconvenient or distasteful? Americans have always been sensitive to the moral implications of what we do abroad. We want to do what is "right." But conflicting principles may be operative in the same problem. Moreover, in a world of finite resources, increasingly interdependent and increasingly dangerous, we cannot pursue our own national interests if we perceive them as entirely selfish, independent of the interests of our allies, or of our enemies. How successfully we sort out these ambivalences and ambiguities will be the mark of our evolution as a nation.

11 / CULTURAL BARRIERS TO INTERNATIONAL UNDERSTANDING

THE LECTURE CIRCUIT acquainted me with the American people in ways that twenty years of foreign service never could. Particularly in the question-and-answer period, I was impressed with the maturity of view evident in many. At the same time, I encountered considerable moral confusion, and cultural barriers to international understanding. In this chapter, I propose to discuss four such barriers.

One of these we may refer to as the self-assertive. In the spring of 1985, in the course of lecturing at American Embassies in Europe, I was told by a senior officer: "More and more, in order to survive in today's Foreign Service, I find myself underplaying my string section and stressing my brass section." I asked him what he meant. "The Foreign Service is changing," he replied. "We are becoming militarized, seeking to enforce American policy on others rather than, by appealing to the hopes and expectations of others, as you recommend, attracting them to follow it." As we have discussed, among the marks of mature judgment is the recognition that others may have a point of view worth respecting. That recognition forms the basis for cooperation, negotiation, and peace-making.

Force and flexibility work in tandem. But stressing our brass section almost to the exclusion of our strings is a step backward on the road to national maturity.

As the economic historian Robert Heilbronner says in his introduction to *The Worldly Philosophers:* "It is only because man is a socially cooperative creature that he has succeeded in perpetuating himself at all. But the very fact that he has to depend on his fellow man has made the problem of survival extraordinarily difficult. Man is not an ant, conveniently equipped with an in-born pattern of social instincts. On the contrary, he seems to be equipped with a fiercely self-centered nature. If his relatively weak physique forces him to seek cooperation, his untamed inner drives constantly threaten to disrupt his social working partnership." Our culture, which emphasizes both cooperation and self-assertiveness, seems to have great difficulty putting the two together. We suffer from a deep ambivalence. On the one hand, our children are told to learn team spirit, how to get along with others. Later in life, team playing becomes a distinct asset in the race for corporate advancement. The successful business deal which depends on each side feeling that it has come out ahead demands respect for another's interests and point of view; in short, the ability to compromise. At the same time, we want our offspring to excel, to get A's or be captain of the team. Later, they hope to be successful in terms of getting ahead. These attitudes and practices, ingrained in our culture, are directly opposed to compromise. Even our legal procedures sanction adversarial attitudes. In his annual report for 1983, Derek Bok, the president of Harvard, criticized the way American lawyers are trained—"in confrontation and conflict, and not in the gentler arts of conflict resolution and accommodation."

No characterization is worse to American ears than "loser." We are brought up to be winners. When, for example, our children come home after participating in an athletic event, what is the first question we ask? Is it: "How well did you play the game?" or, more likely: "Did you win?" Properly channeled, the drive to win and the fear of losing can produce excellence in every field. Improperly applied, they can lead to less than constructive ends. In foreign affairs, such drives and fears impelled Lyndon Johnson to prolong American military intervention in Vietnam lest he be accused of "losing" Vietnam the way a predecessor had "lost" China, of being the first President to lose a war. Americans generally see foreign affairs in terms of winning or losing—in the words of a noted psychiatrist, as "planting Old Glory on top of Mount Suribachi." Until Vietnam, we had won all our wars. Moreover, we engaged in two world wars for what we regard as the best of motives. However, the "win" ethics creates obstacles to a mature view of our international obligations. For we may well have reached a moment in history when we can no longer "win" as we were brought up to think. We owe it to ourselves, and to the world, to be successful in the defense of interests we consider vital. But, increasingly, we must be more selective in determining what these interests are.

Self-assertiveness can be the enemy of national consensus, of broad agreement on national priorities and how they are to be pursued. We seem at times to have a foreign policy based not on consensus but on an agglomeration of interests—individual, ethnic, governmental, commercial—in which the most assertive interest enjoys undue advantage. Obviously, in a democratic, pluralistic society there is no more difficult task than to achieve consensus. Peace-making begins not with the Soviets or any other nation but among ourselves and within each of us. It demands a willingness to respect the interests of others as well as our own, and to acknowledge a larger interest to which individual concerns are subordinate.

Related to the self-assertive in our culture is the isolationist. Its roots vary, beginning with the voyage from the Old World to the New by immigrants who turned their backs on Europe. Two vast oceans made isolation easy to maintain. Our concern for international security became so minimal after the Civil War that the Navy debated reverting from steam to sail, because sail was cleaner. Our national concerns were domestic and we devoted ourselves to developing our vast resources. Throughout the post-Civil War period, and culminating in the years around the First World War, isolationism was reinforced by fear on the part of America's "native stock," white Anglo-Saxon Protestants, of the consequences of large-scale non-English-speaking immigration. Not only might the native stock be diluted, the argument went, but the allegiance of these "hyphenated" Americans was thought to be mixed at best. Thus, Colonel House, President Wilson's confidential adviser, recorded in his diary the following conversation with Wilson's Secretary of State, Robert Lansing:

> I spoke of my advice to the President as to making "Americanism" the main issue of the 1916 campaign. [Lansing] was heartily in favor of it, and he even goes so far as to say that we should restrict immigration for many years until we have assimilated what we already have, and he was in favor of discontinuing the teaching of German and French in our public schools.

The learning of languages, in the wake of World War I, was outlawed in public schools in certain states. Our Foreign Service, certainly among major nations, is the only one that cannot count on its applicants being fluent in at least one foreign language. By 1945, when, after two world wars, it became clear that we could no longer afford to isolate ourselves politically, economically, or militarily from the rest of the world, we still had not outgrown our isolationist psychology. Having held ourselves aloof from other cultures, we assumed our experience to be of universal validity. Indeed, having assimilated and "naturalized" millions of immigrants from various cultural milieus, we thought the rest of the world wanted to be like us. Those like the Shah of Iran who attempted to modernize their countries American-style were vigorously applauded. We projected a world in our own image, where we could be in control or at least feel at home.

Impatient with the complexities of "abroad," we tend to export "made in America" solutions, often on a scale appropriate only in America. The Americanization of the war in Vietnam is only one example. Worse yet, our analyses of overseas problems are too often based on abstraction—what the problem should be, rather than what it really is. We indulge ourselves in the luxury of seeing what we want to see and denying what we do not want to see. On January 1, 1978, for example, on a stopover in Tehran, President Carter toasted the Shah's Iran as an "island of stability" in the Middle East.

Former Secretary of State Cyrus Vance, who accompanied President Carter to Tehran, comments in his book *Hard Choices*: "At the time, [the toast] seemed just the usual effusiveness typical of such situations, and certainly not markedly inconsistent with the prevailing intelligence and academic estimates about the internal situation in Iran." Were they all totally wrong? In October 1979, an Embassy colleague who had served there earlier told me: "In 1977, many of us were aware that something was wrong, that the regime in the way it was going could not last forever." Yet, not until November 9, 1978, did Ambassador William Sullivan in Tehran, in his telegram "Thinking the Unthinkable," come to grips with the possibility of the fall of the Shah. Those reporting officers in the field who, much earlier, had begun to suspect the unthinkable were faced with the reality that if they reported their suspicions, no one in Washington would have taken them seriously. Hence, no Foreign Service or CIA reporting officer, or, according to Vance, no academic, looked for or was willing to see evidence that would in fact reduce his credibility. American expectations determined not only what the conclusions of any report would be but what evidence would be selected to back them.

But government officials, or academics, are not the only offenders. On the lecture circuit, I met a young woman who had just returned from a year of volunteer work among the poor in Nicaragua and who had completed a number of speaking engagements before peace groups in New England. She described how her audiences were simply unwilling to hear anything unfavorable about the Sandinista regime, onto which they had projected their own liberal expectations. The problem is not one of better-informed government officials or academicians versus less-informed peace people. The problem is not professional but cultural. And the danger of living to the extent that we do in a world of our own projection is all the more acute when we deal with the Third World, which is so very different from our own.

Our isolationist inheritance is also a moralistic one. The term is related, obviously, to "moral," and the one can shade into the other. But if "moral" implies responsible living and the ideals that guide it, "moralistic" conveys a judgmental attitude, of believing one's standards to be superior to those of others, of criticizing others on the basis of standards that may not be appropriate to them. From the beginning, Americans have been possessed of a special mission. We saw ourselves as the last best hope of mankind; we envisioned ourselves as the city set on a hill; our expansion across a vast continent was not merely land acquisition but manifest destiny. The great isolationists of the period that ended with World War II, Robert La Follette and Robert A. Taft, justified their position on the grounds that the precious and unique thing that was America could be safeguarded from corrupting influence from abroad only by isolation.

Given our belief in America's God-given destiny, it was easy to assume that what was right for us was right for everyone. Worse, there has been throughout this century a preachy tone in our pronouncements to the world. George Kennan has described it as "a histrionic note—a note of self-consciousness, pretension. There was a desire not just to be something but to appear as something. It was inconceivable that any war in which we were engaged could be less than momentous and decisive for the future of mankind." Our self-righteousness was deepened by two world wars, at the end of which we emerged from isolation. The Allied cause in World War I was perceived as deeply righteous, and the Huns were considered depraved. During World War II, the evil represented by the Nazi regime and the cruelties perpetrated by the Japanese also gave a moral coloration to our war effort. In both wars, our participation, as Kennan noted, had to be justified in moral terms and also by a vision of an idealized, utopian world to follow.

These expectations are most readily seen in the Wilsonian concept of making the world safe for democracy. Emerging from isolation to fight World War I, we, "the last best hope of mankind," risked moral contamination; the world had to be sanitized according to our standards. Moreover, because we believed our purposes to be moral, whatever we did had to be "right." Until Vietnam, we had always managed to win our wars; we and virtue triumphed together, and it was tempting to believe that we triumphed because we were virtuous. So long as our capacity to enforce our view of the good was not challenged, we did not question the rectitude of our aims or the propriety of the means used to attain them. Vietnam raised serious doubts, not only about the propriety of our means but also about our capacity to refashion the world in our own image. And continuing encounters with Middle East terrorism have given us further pause. In these cases, television brought the issues right into the American living room, and our sense of rectitude and our self-confidence as a nation were seriously shaken. Indeed, in the case of the Tehran hostages, our traditional moral arrogance had to be overcome before official Washington could negotiate. In the Council on Foreign Relations study, *American Hostages in Iran*, Harold Saunders describes two prevailing schools of thought:

> One school of thought started from the premise that the authorities in Tehran, however disorganized, had to be held responsible for their acts. Because they constituted themselves as a government of Iran, they had to be made to see, through a variety of pressures, that interests important to them would be damaged if they continued to hold the hostages. With that premise in mind, the discussion focused on more or less traditional . . . means of increasing pressure on Iran. Those who leaned toward this position tended initially to be those . . . whose experience in dealing with other political systems abroad was limited.
>
> Other members of the team . . . felt that a solution would have to provide Iranian leaders with some development to justify releasing the hostages. They started from three thoughts. 1) Whatever the correctness of holding the revolutionary authorities accountable before international law and opinion, the political fact was that the revolution in Iran was still in process . . . The hostages were a weapon in the power struggle. 2) The priorities of the revolutionary leaders started with consolidating the revolution, not with meeting Iran's international responsibilities . . . In any case, revolutionary Iran did not define Iran's responsibilities in terms of Western law and morality, which themselves were targets of the revolution. 3) Whatever steps might be necessary to increase pressure on Iran . . . it would also be necessary to play into the political dynamics of Iran in ways that might generate internal arguments for the release of the hostages . . .

The first school thought of moral responsibility in purely American terms. Fortunately, the second school prevailed.

Finally, among obstacles to international understanding, there is the religiose. I encountered it at the Cathedral of St. John the Divine, when certain clergy ascribed their liberal politics to divine intent. Whenever such religious ascription occurs, politics of whatever description, "right" or "left," can become particularly virulent. Europe's crusades and holy wars, the Ayatollah in his Iranian manifestations, are only too familiar. "He who has Islam has the Truth," Hassan used to remind us. "Of course, Christians must love their enemies," a Protestant leader in Northern Ireland is supposed to have said, "but those Roman Catholics are God's enemies!"

In American society, this crusader instinct does not normally take the form of violence. It persists, nevertheless, in the form of "true belief," the definition and advocacy of views on secular issues with an absolute certainty more appropriate to the basic tenets of revealed religion. True belief in this sense obstructs international understanding, its effects apparent in hawk and dove alike, but, to the public mind, more obvious among the hawks. True belief infuses civic religion, that very American admixture of religious metaphors and nationalistic aspirations, of piety and patriotism. *Annuit Coeptis*, the Latin motto on the reverse of the Great Seal of the United States, is usually translated as: "God has ordained [or, alternatively, favored] our undertakings." It would be comforting to think that most Americans have outgrown such religiosity, that they are willing to concede that God might have His own plan for the world unfettered by the United States Constitution or the two-party system. As Abraham Lincoln pointed out, the Confederates prayed to the same God as did the North. He reminds us that we must do "the right," but we can do that only to the limited extent that God gives us to see it.

Yet both the Reagan Administration and the fundamentalist clergy often act as mouthpieces for the Ayatollah we have described. America's manifest destiny is divinely ordained and messianic; our military establishment is God's terrible swift sword; and our positions are non-negotiable. On such logic, the religious right attacked Secretary of State Shultz for his very success in negotiating the release of the TWA hostages: one does not compromise with the devil. Moral confusion and cultural barriers still interpenetrate to impede our growing up internationally. No less than the attitudes I encountered at the Cathedral of St. John the Divine, and in all of us, they reflect the same Ayatollah. Nor can we deal dispassionately and effectively with terrorists or others who delude themselves that they are God's chosen instruments, so long as we remain prey to the same delusions ourselves.

12 / COPING
WITH TERRORISM

ON JANUARY 16, 1983, four former hostages—Bruce Laingen, Barry Rosen, John Limbert, and I—attended a seminar at Brooklyn College to mark the second anniversary of our release from captivity. We had not seen one another for some time, and had not discussed what we planned to say. Yet our conclusions, reported in *The New York Times*, were remarkably similar. Each of us said that his interest in Iranian society and affairs had been undiminished by his captivity. Our major disappointment was the widespread failure to deal with its lessons. "Many people in and out of government," Bruce Laingen observed, "would like to put it all aside and just say, 'Thank God it's over.'" Laingen continued, "We Americans are sometimes insensitive to the impact of our culture abroad, particularly on traditional cultures undergoing rapid change."

After the meeting was thrown open for questions, Dr. Herbert Tepper, a retired teacher, berated us for "condoning" the conduct of our captors. "I cannot but feel that you people are taking too kind a view of the situation," Tepper concluded. "We're not making excuses for them," Barry Rosen replied, "but there is reason to think that the Iranians have had a social revolution of great profundity. It was clearly one of the most broad-range revolutions of the twentieth century." Laingen stressed the difference between not condoning the conduct of our captors and understanding their motives. Without first understanding terrorists, one cannot begin to deal with the problem of terrorism. "If," I added, "we allow our natural resentment to color our dispassionate view of who these people are, and what their motives were, then we weaken our chances of understanding the problem."

Other returning hostages—most notably, many of the passengers from TWA 847, and Jeremy Levin, the former Middle East bureau chief for Cable News Network, who was kidnapped in Beirut and held hostage by Lebanese Shiites for eleven months—have expressed much the same view. Their conclusions, which, admittedly, not all returning hostages share, are contrary to what the circumstances of their captivities might be expected to generate.

What *did* happen to so many of us? It was not, as many TV interviewers would have us believe, the result of Stockholm Syndrome, the condition in which captives identify with their captors and side with them against their liberators. Nor were my responses, vituperative critics to the contrary, based on anti-Israeli sentiment. A call for American evenhandedness in the interest of a lasting peace in the Middle East, which includes the security of Israel, is quite something else. For me, the beginning of the answer surfaced at the hostage reunion at the Greenbrier in April 1981, when the keynote speaker reminded us that, as a result of a death-threatening experience, we had caught a glimpse of our real selves. By analogy, to the extent that many of us, when taken captive, may have held a somewhat idealized view of "abroad," or projected American experience as if it were universally applicable, the hostage experience forced us to confront Iranian reality. If, to continue Barry Rosen's thought, that experience was a by-product of a "social revolution of great profundity," it induced in a number of us an equally profound psychological revolution. Even in captivity, I had begun to wonder by what means a similar and overdue revolution might be induced in the thinking of our fellow Americans.

In bringing about any change of attitude, the first and indispensable step is to persuade people that a shift is necessary. Some Americans still deny that it is, because our economic and military power is overwhelming, and our value system and national resolve strong. But in the years to come, we will have no real defense against terrorism except through a revolution in our thinking, and the new attitude and behavior that should result. For at least another generation, we will be facing a threat of Middle East terrorism. We cannot control it. Nor can we abandon an area we can no longer control. Our interests in the Middle East are too important. So we must hang in, highly vulnerable to terrorist action, while terrorists offer few if any targets for retaliation. Furthermore, the Middle East terrorist has learned to use major components of American power to turn our once comfortable assumptions about ourselves and our role in the world upside down. Our technical prowess, from which much of our nation's pride in itself, its military and economic strength, and its standard of living have been derived, makes us especially vulnerable. For example, the United States is responsible, more than any other nation, for the ease and rapidity of international travel, which provides targets and hostages for terrorist action. In our society, electricity and gas are brought to large urban centers by conduits easy to demolish. Our urban centers themselves are potential hostages. We cannot post guards at every pylon of every power grid, or along every gas pipeline, or, for that matter, in every subway tunnel. We cannot body-search every passenger on every domestic flight.

Electronic communication delivers terrorism's message, as

it has that of the forces arrayed against us and against Israel for the past thirty years. The transistor radio in the 1950s carried Nasser's inflammatory words to virtually every Arab between Morocco and the Persian Gulf. In Paris, the Ayatollah Khomeini taped his sermons so that the direct-dial telephone system provided for the Shah by AT&T and GTE could transmit his call to revolution; it was relayed to every mosque and broadcast to the faithful throughout Iran. Worldwide television brought our captors into every American home, and made the nation hostage to Iran. The consequences of concerted and sustained terrorist action would, of course, be appalling. And there may be other, more far-reaching consequences. In its efforts to defend itself against terrorism, our government may be tempted to place arbitrary restrictions on civil rights; the democratic process and the rule of law may be seriously weakened. My private nightmare is that of a mindless popular belief that Israel is exclusively responsible for Palestinian terrorism; this could lead to a recrudescence of anti-Semitism which could poison our entire society.

What can we do to protect ourselves, and our allies? I foresee a multifaceted defense, beginning with improved passive security measures and active military and covert measures. The Israelis have been most successful in penetrating the Palestine Liberation Organization. Palestinian terrorist groups are far from united. Playing one off against the other is not impossible. The Soviets reportedly made effective use of Walid Jumblatt, their Lebanese Druze ally, in their successful recovery of three of their four kidnapped diplomats. Selective assassination of terrorist leaders should not be ruled out, always provided that this can be done cleanly and deniably. With innocent lives at stake, we cannot be too squeamish.

At the same time, we must be scrupulous and discerning in deciding when and how to use such means. We should apply the criteria of "just war," which since the fifth century have identified for Western civilization those situations in which resort to arms is justified. We cannot be indiscriminate in the way we retaliate; innocent bystanders must be protected, lest we increase and consolidate support for the terrorists. Similarly, the retaliation must be proportionate to the injury inflicted, lest we become like the terrorists. Most important, when we seek out terrorists to destroy them, there must be a high probability of success, or we will look like fools.

Our best defense, however, is our own maturity, our basic resolve, our patience, and our capacity for sacrifice. These qualities we particularly need to draw on when terrorists make unacceptable demands. Although I personally have experienced the despair that the four Americans now held by Lebanese Shiites must be feeling, there is no way that the U.S. government can meet the demands of their captors. Pressuring the Kuwaiti government to release the Shiite terrorists tried and convicted of blowing up the French and American embassies there in December 1983 would undercut the credibility of our efforts to combat terrorism, and put other lives at risk.

The real test of our nation's maturity, however, will be how soon we accept the reality that no measures, technical, military, or covert, however effective, can afford more than temporary or symptomatic relief. A nation that experienced the satisfaction of the Navy's interception of the aircraft carrying the Palestinian hijackers of the cruise ship *Achille Lauro*, in October 1985, in the very next month witnessed another hijacking, this time of an airliner, and later, massacres at two major airports. In reprisal, we may bring quite a few Middle East terrorists to justice, or extinction. But other terrorists quickly step up to take their place. Israel's policy of instant retaliation has not brought Middle East terrorism to an end. Measures that do not address underlying causes only raise false hopes. They only delay the moment when the nation will have to realign its thinking.

Let us begin that realignment by not giving way to moral outrage. We should be angry when innocent Americans are killed, injured, or taken hostage. But moral outrage at means that we have not hesitated to use, or support or tolerate in others, only suggests the extent of our moral confusion, our hypocrisy. Some argue, for example, that indiscriminate killing of innocent people by a state in pursuit of its national interests, while regrettable, is at least tolerable, whereas indiscriminate killing by splinter groups and subnational groups, such as the Palestinians in pursuit of their national interests, is to be condemned. That line of argument looks like a Catch-22 to Palestinians who want a state of their own. Above all, moral outrage weakens our capacity for objectivity and clouds the sharpness of our perception. Moral outrage renders us less able to address the problem, and when it inspires bluster and threats that the world knows will not be carried out or action against surrogate targets like the Libyan Navy, our effectiveness is all the more impaired.

Terrorism gives rise to conceptual as well as moral confusion. Some people have urged that terrorism itself be considered a crime and its perpetrators punished accordingly. They forget that giving terrorism a legal status different from that of common criminal acts dignifies terrorism and furnishes a justification for murder, arson, and other crimes. In this connection, American judges have turned down British requests for the extradition of gunmen from the Irish Republican Army. Our judges rely on a clause in our extradition treaty with Britain exempting from extradition crimes such as murder if they can be classified as "political offenses." A treaty is the law of the land. In effect, this one with Great Britain protests murderers, arsonists, and burglars, so long as their motives are political. Criminal action, justified by political motive, is one definition of terrorism.

Before "declaring war on terrorism," to cite one of the slogans of the morally outraged, it might be useful to identify what we are supposed to war against. Confusion shines forth in such documents as U.S. Senate Resolution 186 of July 11, 1985, introduced by Senator Alfonse M. D'Amato of New York, which calls for a treaty to "prevent and respond to terrorism." Along with some very useful provisions, including more effective international coordination of intelligence operations and uniform laws on asylum and extradition, the proposal would "create an internationally accepted definition of terrorism." In December 1984, I participated in a conference in England on the subject of terrorism. In a blue-ribbon international group including senior officials from Scotland Yard and the FBI, politicians, luminaries from the media, and academic experts, I was the token hostage. We wasted an entire morning unsuccessfully trying to hammer out an acceptable definition of terrorism, only to take refuge in Clement Attlee's "an elephant is hard to define, but if one comes into the room, you know damn well what it is."

Confusion about how to define a terrorist leads those in church and peace groups who sentimentalize whatever comes out of the Third World to argue that some of those whom today we call terrorists may in time be known as freedom fighters. Ultimately, the argument continues, today's terrorists may be hailed as statesmen and peacemakers. Former President Jomo Kenyatta of Kenya and former Prime Minister Menachem Begin of Israel were once terrorists. From this, it is argued that we should be "understanding" and shrink from taking the strongest possible measures against terrorists. Certainly, being a terrorist is no guarantee of winning a Nobel Peace Prize. I believe we should let the future make its own judgments, and defend ourselves as best we can today. Although the actions were taken by governments and not small groups, I am reminded of World War II, in which German U-boat captains were cowardly because they "attacked unarmed merchant ships," whereas brave U.S. submarine commanders "swept the seas of Jap shipping."

We can, however, make a real distinction between those irregular or subnational groups which serve our national interests and those which oppose them. The same realism should lead us to question what national interest is served by our consistent refusal to recognize the national identity and rights of the Palestinian people. Israel's future security, as well as our own, demands that we extend to the Palestinian people, through their representatives in the Palestine Liberation Organization, the recognition that Israel demands for itself. This is not "caving in" before terrorism. Rather, it responds to the hope always held out by the moderate Palestinians, that justice will prevail. When that hope becomes credible, extremists lose their credibility, and terrorism over time its perceived necessity. It will, of course, take years to integrate a generation of radicalized Palestinian youth into peaceful pursuits. But that is all the more reason to begin the peace process right away.

At the same time, we cannot deceive ourselves that progress on the Palestinian front will end the threat of terrorism by the Third World. Other developing nations have fundamental concerns, often economic in nature, to which the United States has been less than responsive. A leading member of the PLO has pointed out that the Palestinians are only precursors. Others, whose grievances may be economic rather than political, will learn to "play the terrorist card," until their grievances are addressed. "If," he reportedly said, "the Americans don't care, we'll make them care." Our younger captors expected, prematurely as it turned out, that their revolution, and their actions against us, would spark uprisings by the poor and oppressed elsewhere in the Third World. Certainly, much of that world has been observing the Middle East closely. The issue is broader, therefore, than the Palestinians, or the Middle

East, or even the Third World. It is how to stimulate Americans to change, in order better to understand and deal with these emerging forces. The battle against terrorism ultimately will have to be fought in our own minds. It can be won only by a change of attitude. Fear inspired by terrorism will be a primary catalyst, and paradoxically, by compelling Americans to respond to its challenge in these broader dimensions, Middle East terrorism will undermine its own raison d'être. Yet fear, without wisdom, is not a reliable guide. As we saw with the Nuclear Freeze, fear can stimulate a consciousness of the need for change, but it does not necessarily lead to sound directions for change, or set practical goals, or show citizens how to achieve them. Indeed, fear could produce anger, demands for action to relieve frustration, and an escalation of violence to the point where lasting solutions become harder and harder to achieve.

The Nuclear Freeze campaign was triggered by widespread apprehension that the Reagan Administration was not taking nuclear disarmament seriously enough. Essentially, the Freeze was a call for new ideas in dealing with the Soviets. A paucity of inspiration still seems to characterize the U.S. government in its efforts to deal with Middle East terrorism. Is there a possibility of stimulating popular demand for new approaches? The challenge is awesome. The Council for International Understanding, which I direct, was established in May 1983 to explore ways to rethink our attitudes about ourselves and foreign affairs. Its principal efforts are focused on two major agents of change in American society: schools and churches.

Schools have been basic to the Americanization of millions of immigrants. Landmark Supreme Court decisions singled out the public school as the institution most influential in forming racial attitudes; and the Court insisted that schools take the leading role in the desegregation of American society. Today the American educational establishment is also turning with verve and imagination to deal with inadequacies in the nation's understanding of its international responsibilities. Yet educators, like the rest of us, can fall victim to outworn paradigms. "International education" tends to be conceived of in terms of traditional curricula, merely stepping up the transmittal of information about "abroad," along with the hours devoted to language training. Of course, such measures are essential. The level of competence in foreign languages in our society is very low indeed. Our knowledge of geography is shockingly poor. Hossein Sheikholeslam commented to me that most of his classmates at Berkeley did not know where Iran was. But these measures are not enough. I do not see in study plans for "global awareness" much attention paid to dealing with the students' cultural biases, which determine how they will interpret what they learn. The teaching of our history tends to perpetuate our world view, our myths, our confusion between American policy and divine intent. What is taught may only nurture prejudice and reinforce erroneous conclusions. A senior official at SUNY, the State University of New York, has described to me how, in his judgment, a new high-school syllabus for African studies is likely to reinforce the traditional American stereotypes about Africa that the students bring with them to class.

Similarly, I do not see enough attention paid in "international" curricula to problems of moral confusion. Over the years, public education has deluded itself with the belief that it is value-free. (Of course, that assumption itself represents a value judgment.) But, in any case, the development of the capacity to make moral judgments tended to be excluded. The results were brought home to me in 1983 when I served on a panel discussing nuclear education for the New York City public-school system. My remarks, later published under the title "Trained to Be Terrorized," criticized a new textbook prepared by science teachers which analyzed students' chances of survival in the event of a nuclear attack on Manhattan. Since those chances are nil, the text only increased the tension and fear that the nuclear education program was intended to alleviate. The political dimension, including the causes of Soviet–American confrontation, and differences that could be negotiated, was not touched upon. The moral dimension of nuclear warfare, or of foreign affairs generally, was to play no role in the education of New York's future citizens.

Fortunately, the problems inherent in "value-free" education have been recognized. "Critical values" on the personal level are being introduced into high-school and community-college teaching. So far as I know, problems of ethics and values have not generally been introduced into global issues. It is interesting that in dealing with international affairs, rather than with personal concerns, students are less likely to be self-conscious about discussing values. Once students begin to deal with values, the questions and problems can then be redirected to their personal concerns.

International education, as presently conceived, suffers from a further disadvantage; it relies too much on the intellectual grasp of the subject, on the cognitive as opposed to the intuitive. Both play an important role in the shaping and shifting of attitudes. However, the intuitive side, developed by experience, may well be the more important. It was not mandatory courses in cultural anthropology or sociology which the United States Supreme Court ordered when it required the desegregation of our public schools. Rather, it was the experience of "rubbing shoulders," the daily contact with those of another cultural background which was counted on to stimulate change and improved interracial understanding. We can see in Miami daily interaction and growing symbiosis of Hispanic and Anglo cultures, de facto international and intercultural understanding arrived at through shared everyday experience. Although I prided myself on my academic knowledge of the Middle East before I joined the Foreign Service, I never really began to understand the area until I served there. My captivity distilled my prior experience and enabled me to draw conclusions from it.

Thus, the best educational environment would, in theory, be overseas. The many programs that enable an American student to live with a family for a summer or to pursue an academic year abroad can be very enlightening. Mature, naturally perceptive students benefit from such experience. But international understanding does not result automatically from a stay abroad. At the end of the First World War, many Norwegian families took in Austrian and German children threatened with malnutrition as a result of the Allied blockade. Some of these same children, by 1940 of military age, were used to spearhead the German occupation of Norway in World War II. What Norwegians found hardest to comprehend or forgive was that the young German soldiers couldn't understand why they weren't welcomed by their former foster parents. Turning most students loose in a foreign environment without adequate preparation, in the hope that they will develop international understanding would be not unlike turning them loose in a library without mentors, reading lists, and tests to measure accomplishment, in the hope that, on their own, they might read and improve their minds.

However instructive a "living abroad" program may be, that experience is not likely to rub off on the students who don't go abroad. Indeed, the more a student is immersed in the experience of living and studying abroad, the more the experience is likely to have altered his or her outlook. Returning students often find themselves isolated from their classmates who stayed home. "Hey, where did you go last year? France, huh! Say, how *was* it?" But those who ask such questions rarely want an answer.

In the face of these numerous difficulties, American educators are coming up with innovative programs with a very high potential for altering popular attitudes about "abroad." One example is the Partnership for Service-Learning, a consortium of colleges, service agencies, churches, and related organizations of which CIU is a charter member. Combining the cognitive/intellectual with the intuitive/experiential, Service-Learning joins rigorous academic study with work experience in a cross-cultural setting. The service portion, which can include providing health care, tutoring in reading, mathematics, or vocational skills, supervising recreation or organizing community development, builds the experience to which the academic process can meaningfully be related. Having made a success of its pilot programs in Ghana and England in 1983, the Partnership is now concentrating on the Third World. There are programs lasting a summer, a semester, or a year in Jamaica, Ecuador, and the Philippines. By 1987, programs will be under way in Israel.

When foreign cultures are not merely studied but their different assumptions are dealt with in the workplace, and, similarly, when hitherto unquestioned values are challenged and tested, the student is compelled to self-examination and reappraisal. Work experience is related to academic discipline through individual study under a qualified local teacher. The student keeps a personal journal, which is evaluated locally and returned to the student's home campus for final marking. We must carefully define and identify the cultural biases that students bring to the program, and evaluate the effectiveness of the student's overseas experience in correcting them. CIU is also investigating ways to tap the American students' experience abroad, as well as that of the foreign students on our campuses, for the benefit of students who cannot go abroad. Beyond that, we are looking into ways by which, drawing on all these assets, colleges and universities can project greater understanding of the developing world onto their communities.

CIU is also exploring the possibility of computer simulation programs based on the Iranian hostage crisis. The programs will combine high drama and human interest—the great concern with terrorism, and the students' fascination with computer technology. The "players" would be required to make and live with decisions that could result in a number of different outcomes. To the extent possible, we will incorporate into the software different ethical and cultural assumptions that the players must deal with. Admittedly, the binary, black-and-white logic of the computer is not intrinsically well suited to dealing with ambiguity, ambivalence, paradox, and all the gray areas we have been discussing. The computer excels, however, at forcing the player to make decisions and confront the results; if you decide to do this, you may no longer be able to do that—which is fundamental to international affairs.

CIU is also working closely with organized religion—churches, synagogues, ethical culture societies, ashrams—which is a major force, particularly for those of more mature years. To take one example, CIU has contracted with the Episcopal Church Center in New York, and the Episcopal Radio-TV Foundation in Atlanta, to make a series of twelve-minute videotapes for the use of adult study forums throughout the Episcopal Church. Each will consist of an interview with me, the congregation of Atlanta's Church of the Holy Innocents providing audience reaction. Much of the subject matter will be drawn from this book. The project grew out of a memorandum I submitted in September 1985 to the Episcopal Church Center, entitled "How will the Episcopal Church respond to terrorism?" After describing the monastic retreat referred to in chapter 9, I went on to point out:

The experiential approach recognizes that the basic difficulty of most Episcopalians in understanding foreign
affairs arises not from lack of information as much as
from faulty attitudes. Becoming an effective Christian
citizen demands self-examination and self-understanding
as a basis for understanding others, and for interaction
with them. We learn to cope with ambiguity and, by
integrating seeming opposites, to live with paradox. In
short, this is part of the growing-up process that we all
have to go through individually in our own lives, and as
a nation in foreign affairs. And growing up is something
that cannot be learned academically. Somehow, it must
be experienced. Our solution is to transmit experience
vicariously

—by encouraging adults in study forums to relate to a
role model who has gone through a significant experience with which they can identify;

—to draw conclusions from that experience; for their
own lives and for their understanding of foreign
affairs.

Accordingly, each videotape will be accompanied by an instruction kit for the group leader of the adult study forum, to
help him or her draw out the complementary experience of
the participants, and to draw conclusions at the end.

Quite obviously, no single such meeting, and no series, can
generate the intensity I found in the monastic retreat, much
less the pressures of the hostage experience. But such meetings can establish directions for attitudinal change which
religious organizations, in the context of their whole mission,
of worship, of scripture, and quest for justice and peace, can
then stimulate and reinforce. For these purposes, nothing can
quite take the place of preaching. On October 6, 1985, I delivered the sermon at All Saints' Church in Brookline, Massachusetts. We processed in, singing, "Blessing abound where'er
He reigns, / The prisoner leaps to loose his chains . . ." Surely,

I thought, this is clerical tact at its finest. Beyond that, the occasion showed how broad and inclusive the church, at its best, can be. While I was a Foreign Service officer, the rector, the Reverend Nathaniel Pierce, was arrested and imprisoned for his extreme peace activities. Yet, for all our differences of style and view, Nat felt that his congregation should hear what I had to say. From the pulpit, I reminded the congregation that during the TWA hijacking the previous summer I had tried to persuade television audiences and others of the importance of understanding the terrorist. Yet no one in the Episcopal Church had publicly expressed support for this eminently Christian position. To Episcopalians, the Third World is populated exclusively by men such as Bishop Tutu, who respond nobly to oppression by those of European descent. How, then, was our church to react when the Third World reared up and began to oppress Americans? Since that did not fit the stereotype, the Episcopal Church had little to say and, probably wisely, remained silent. Perhaps someday we may develop a concept broad enough to embrace all abuses of human rights, including those suffered by Americans?

It is so easy to be against socially undesirable things, to address problems that are safe, or chic, or remote. Nobody likes apartheid. Nobody wants to send Americans to die in Central America, and nobody really loves the bomb. But when a stance is unpopular, as mine certainly was, then you don't find false heroics coming out of the church. Rather, the church prefers to allow the media to determine the issues upon which it will pronounce. When the shooting gets loud enough in El Salvador or Nicaragua to make good television, though, you can be sure that there will be a corresponding noise coming out of the pulpit—but not before, and not afterward. Only when it's topical. At such times, the church comes out at its negative worst. "Stop making nuclear weapons"—

of course, we all would like to see that—but not "What kind of world order should we be pursuing that will take the place of the present mutual terror?" "Ban investment in South Africa," but not "What kind of multiracial South Africa should we be prepared to support; and what are the dangers that we see, assuming that apartheid is brought to an end, because it's not going to be an easy time." Or again, of course, "End aid to the contras in Nicaragua," but not "What kind of Central America will afford security and decency of life to its people?"

We, the church, I continued, are not involved on a hands-on basis in the running of foreign affairs. We can therefore afford to take the long view. Since we can take a long view, we can ask the awkward questions of government as no on else can. The media certainly can't. We have a concept of eternity. We are citizens, not just of our own country, but of another kingdom as well, a kingdom of hope. Ours should be the task of setting goals—for ourselves, for our country, and for the world. How much we church people have going for us, so much insight do the Gospels give us into the motives of mankind! If anybody should, we should understand the forces of evil. And as a practical matter, where else in our society do serious people gather once a week where they can relate their lives to larger questions? I would suggest that our church, any church, does not know its own strength and its own potential. In this area it squanders what strength it has. It cheapens its own currency in trying too often to be relevant. The church loses its authority as a mediator in trying to be a lobby, to be an advocate for the short-term, when we have within us the capacity to stimulate serious, long-term thinking. Let us remember who we are. And so I concluded my talk: Let us not be afraid to go out from this sanctuary, and to say to the rest of the world, "These are issues you must pay attention to." But let us also say, "Now let's just take a minute to ask why, and how, we're going to address them."

In addition to its work with schools and colleges, CIU is initiating a program for business organizations. None of these institutional agents of change, however, can be more than intermediaries. Ultimately, change must occur within the individual citizen.

AFTERWORD

by Louisa Kennedy

ON MONDAY, DECEMBER 2, 1985, funeral services were held at St. Ignatius Church in Chestnut Hill, Massachusetts, for William Keough, former hostage. He was fifty-five years old.

Fifteen months earlier, Bill had learned that he was suffering from amyotrophic lateral sclerosis, a degenerative disease of the nervous system, popularly known as Lou Gehrig's disease. He knew that there was no cure and that in time he would be totally dependent. He and his wife, Katherine, knew that he would never teach again or lead a normal, healthy life.

The bitter news for the Keoughs, who along with the other Iranian hostages and their families had been through the unnerving 444 days of captivity in Tehran, must at first have seemed insurmountable. On his return from Iran, Bill had accepted an appointment as an official with the U.S. Department of Education and the Keoughs had established a residence in Washington. Like the rest of us, Katherine and Bill were adjusting to their past experiences. But it seemed too soon, unfair, and incomprehensible that they must face yet another grim vigil. Bill came to grips with the curtailment of his future very quickly. He told Katherine that he had no de-

sire to prolong his illness and that the time they had left together would last only as long as his own bodily resources
would allow. He intended to be at home, in his own bed, when
God called him. His decision obviously reflected a desire not
to put his family through any more distress than was necessary. It was a gallant determination, if difficult to act upon. In
our country, it is very difficult to die at home. Neither the
medical profession nor society is comfortable with death as a
natural event. Doctors resisted treating him unless he agreed to
enter a hospital. Bill persisted, and during the last afternoon
of his life Katherine, protecting his final wish, sat quietly at
his bedside holding his hand. Together they sustained their
privacy and his dignity to the end. Shocked and saddened by
his death, we could not help marveling at the courage, so fitting
in its way, shown by a man who had proved earlier that he
could be a survivor.

Bill had been superintendent of the American School in
Tehran until political events forced it to close in 1979. Files
and equipment from the school were moved to the American Embassy in Iran for safekeeping. Bill was transferred
from Iran to Pakistan, where he took up duties as headmaster
of the American School in Islamabad. Assured by the Embassy in Tehran that there was no danger, Bill returned from
Islamabad to Iran on November 1, 1979, to arrange for the
shipping of student records back to the United States. Bruce
Laingen offered him guest quarters at the Embassy and so,
along with the rest of the Embassy personnel, Bill was taken
hostage.

During the hostage crisis, Katherine Keough became my
closest friend. We shared the ups and downs of a lengthy,
emotional experience, and I was devastated to learn suddenly
in August 1984 that she had a grave and new personal crisis
to face. A week before Bill died, Katherine had a quiet dinner
with us in New York. Determined not to be a professional

widow, she had recently, with Bill's full support, begun teaching again part-time. She now commuted from Washington to New York two days a week. That evening, she shared with us some of her consuming sorrow, but it was clear that once again she had found the means to cope. She told us simply that the earlier crisis had given her great inner strength, that because of it she could confront and deal with everything that came later. Indeed, as she spoke, I was once again with the same courageous person, full of humor and grace, that I had grown to know and value so highly.

In mid-October 1979, Henry Precht, the Country Director for Iran at the Department of State in Washington, had earnestly suggested that it was my duty to join Mike—as my husband is called—at Embassy Tehran. Of course, it was understood that I would have to pay my own way, since the Department was at the moment not flying dependents to Tehran. But he assured me that a part-time job, possibly in the consulate, could be found for me. I informed him rather stiffly that I had a flourishing real-estate business in Washington, and beyond that, my instincts told me that our four sons did not need both parents in Tehran; one there was bad enough. Precht's lip curled contemptuously. He was obviously in no mood to hear any more from me. Containing my anger was difficult. From the beginning, I had had a great uneasiness about Mike's assignment.

I visited the Iran Desk again on Wednesday, October 31, ten days after the Shah was admitted to the United States for medical treatment. Henry Precht was absent, but Mark Johnson, the Deputy Desk Officer, agreed with me that the situation in Iran seemed to be deteriorating rapidly. He showed me a recent report written by my husband which only increased my fears. However, my conclusions were clearly not shared by Arthur, the head of the economic section, just in from Tehran. He described Iran as a very pleasant country to live in and pooh-poohed my reservations. His manner was so bland, he was so sure of his pronouncements, that I remained transfixed: I am astonished even to this day at this officer's ability to gaze into a simmering volcano and see only roses blooming. I spoke to Mike that Wednesday on the direct Embassy–Washington phone line and begged him to take a few days' leave in London. Surely, demonstrators massing at the Embassy gates were hardly conducive to getting any work done, and he was, after all, to celebrate his forty-ninth birthday on Monday, November 5.

On Sunday, November 4, shortly after 7 a.m., I received a telephone call from the State Department. The caller, a friend, broke the news that the Embassy had been taken over by revolutionary students. "No one has been hurt, as far as we know," he said. "The situation isn't clear yet, but come on down." I dressed hurriedly and, not stopping to make breakfast, reached the Operations Center on the seventh floor in less than an hour. When I arrived, members of the Near East Bureau were talking to Bruce Laingen at Iran's Foreign Ministry. I spoke briefly to Laingen and learned that Mike had been at the morning staff meeting and was, Bruce was sure, a captive with the others in the Embassy compound. Although the telephone connection to Bruce was remarkably clear and he managed to make me feel optimistic about a sane and swift resolution to this frightening event, in the days that followed I glared at Henry Precht whenever I could catch his eye.

My chief duty quickly became to man telephones with several Operations Center staffers in order to contact other families. The frenzy was incredible, and the tension palpable. As one day followed the next and my work at the Operations Center gradually became a routine, I was grateful that at least there was something I could do to help relieve the tension of this nightmare. Rita Ode (whose husband, Bob, was also one of the captives) and I were swiftly on a first-name basis with myriad other hostage families through our improvised information channel. The phone bank grew as we were joined within a day or two by Marian Precht, Henry's wife; Betsy Barnes, wife of Harry Barnes, the director general of the Foreign Service; and wives of other Foreign Service officers who volunteered to work eight hours a day to keep in touch with hostage families, to inform, encourage, and comfort them. These women remained at the phones until the day the hostages were released and even several weeks after they returned. Their fidelity to our plight touched me profoundly. Would I have devoted myself to such a duty had I not been personally affected? I rather doubt it. These women personified the spirit of the Foreign Service at its finest.

Seventeen hostage families lived in the Washington metropolitan area, and on November 9, 1979, representatives of these families were invited to the medical offices of the Department to talk with State's doctors and social workers. The purpose was to pool our thoughts and issue a press statement. President Carter, accompanied by Secretary of State Cyrus Vance, made a surprise appearance at our meeting. We took the opportunity to blow off a lot of steam. "What are we going to do now that the horse has left the barn?" I heard myself saying angrily to Mr. Vance, who was quietly outlining events that had led to the takeover. Both men flinched. The moment was painful for everyone. But, on balance, I think this meeting was productive. The personal concern of the President and Mr. Vance was apparent in their deeply lined faces. Their presence helped restore some of our equilibrium.

On Friday, December 7, the State Department held a briefing for all the hostage families. For many, it was the first visit to Washington. Certainly, few had had any firsthand experience with State Department officials. The meeting was held in one of the large conference auditoriums. On the stage were top-ranking White House spokesmen and State Department officials from the Near East Bureau. Each of them spoke at length about the complex problem and how the government was evaluating and proposing to deal with it. The morning briefing was obviously well thought through by these officials, but they were necessarily cautious about anticipating an immediate solution. Their choice of words also implied a certain highhandedness, for they used jargon familiar to Department regulars but largely incomprehensible to outsiders. Implicit in this presentation, too, was the strong suggestion that they preferred a distance kept between themselves and the families. While they promised to keep the families informed, it seemed clear that much information was not to be shared with us. The briefing left many families feeling helpless and outraged. Tempers flared, and tape recordings made during the private briefing were later handed to the press by angry family members reacting to the content and tone of the briefing.

At the afternoon session, the President and the Secretary of State joined the meeting. They talked personally with each family. Mr. Carter told us what he later said in so many words to a congressional group in the East Room of the White House: his first commitment was to protect the interest of the nation—the long-run, long-range interest; the second was to insure the lives and safety of the hostages; third, to secure their release unharmed; fourth, to avoid bloodshed; and fifth, to gain support for the American position from the vast majority of nations on earth. In his remarks, Cyrus Vance concurred with the President's priorities. It was clear to the families that these decent men were concerned with the hostages as human beings and not as elements in a larger political game. As time went on, the majority of the families were able to take a firm and united stand behind the White House.

In retrospect, I see that we learned early the unavoidable and necessary disciplines in the delicate quandary that arises when hostages are taken. Standing behind our country's decisions is important even when one feels the government's thinking is at odds with one's personal interests. Families must recognize that government has priorities other than the safety of individual hostages, and must make that awareness clear to those who have to make the appallingly difficult decisions in such crises. Otherwise, the families will not be effective in their relations with the government. One must remember that, flawed as our institutions may sometimes be, we are fortunate to have them. At perilous times in their history, many nations—such as Iran and Lebanon—have had no institutions working for them at all. When facing difficult decisions, I and others used to ask ourselves an important question: Would our loved ones want to return home if the price of freedom was the impairment of our national integrity?

Shortly after this meeting, I received an invitation from Barbara Walters to be interviewed on ABC News. I hesitated several weeks before accepting the invitation, but finally did. The program aired on December 12. Toward the end of the interview, she pitched me the shocker question: "How would you feel if your husband does not come home?" There it was out in the open, and I had no difficulty phrasing my deeply pondered answer. "Barbara, our country was built on sacrifice," I said. "If that is the way it has to be, I would feel deep pride in my husband and the others." Those may not have been the exact words, but this reaction was one I felt certain my husband and others shared. Later, in their letters home, my husband and many of the other Iranian hostages confirmed my judgment.

The President got through to the families, but, with few exceptions, the attitude of many officials at State remained condescending and was baffling for many families. I find it ironic that at the outset of the crisis it was the Department wives who immediately saw the need for the Department to respect the families' concerns and who stepped quickly into the breach. It is an unfortunate fact that over the years the Department has treated wives of their employees as something akin to free labor. It has adamantly shied away from considering ways to recompense wives adequately for the functions they are expected to perform overseas. New realities are making inroads on this form of chauvinism in the career service, and the Department is at last instituting practices to rectify the situation. Even so, the system moves warily and slowly, and it did so with regard to the human factor inherent in the hostage crisis. I faced ingrained chauvinism not infrequently during the time that I acted as the media spokesperson for the families. Shortly after a 7 a.m. appearance on NBC "Today" show in the fall of 1980, I remember running into a fairly senior officer in a State Department corridor who had seen the program. "How State Department-y you were this morning, Mrs. Kennedy," he remarked dryly, and strode on. I tried not to take this silly comment to heart. There was little time or inclination for that, in face of my wearing schedule. Such insensitivity hurt, however, and I remember it five years later as being a prevalent attitude. After his return, my husband was greeted in State's cafeteria line by another senior official, who remarked in an approving manner: "Look at all your wife and the others accomplished—and straight out of the supermarket!"

After the December briefing at the State Department, hostage families returned to their homes around the country to look for ways to cope with our nightmare. It was not easy for anyone. Each day seemed like a roller-coaster ride through a house of horrors. Fortunately, Americans rarely take things lying down, and before long, family members put aside tears and anger and got down to the business of forming support groups and talking to Iranian diplomats, American clergy, and other intermediaries, who helped us to pry open some channels of communication between the captives and their families. In this informal manner, with the day-to-day encouragement of the volunteers on the Operations Center telephones and the growing support of the American public, we kept our heads and hopes high.

In mid-March of 1980, hopes floundered badly when various government initiatives collapsed. Khomeini then announced that the fate of the hostages would be decided by the Iranian parliament. As this parliament was only in an early stage of formation, hostage family members realized that our vigil might be extended indefinitely. Penne Laingen, the chargé's wife, and I called together the families from the Washington metropolitan area on Saturday, March 22. The time had come, we felt, to create a formal organization through which we could strengthen our group resolve. The acronym FLAG (Family Liaison Action Group) was chosen for its patriotic symbolism. We noted that Old Glory seemed eerily emblematic of the hostages themselves. There were fifty men and women held captive in the Embassy compound, representing the fifty bright stars in the flag. Thirteen Americans, representing its broad stripes, had been released in late 1979, and Bruce Laingen and two colleagues—confined in an upper room of the Iranian Foreign Ministry—symbolized the flag's three colors.

Katherine Keough was the unanimous choice for president of FLAG. She brought to this role humor, quiet strength, and fine administrative abilities. A former professor of demography who had earned her Ed.D. in educational administration, she also represented a different element among the hostage families. With few exceptions, the hostages were either from the ranks of the military or from the Foreign Service. Even in our relatively small organization, feelings of injustice ran high if either group was felt to be overly influential in reaching major decisions.

FLAG's initial meeting was dramatically overshadowed by the prospect of the Shah, then residing in Panama, being readmitted to the United States. To our minds, he chose the better course when that Sunday night he journeyed instead to Egypt. An official invitation to him to return to the United States would have created a serious rift between us and the Administration.

FLAG was an organization that the State Department could readily deal with. With the resources of the Department behind it, and the unstinting support of Sheldon Keys, Executive Director of the Near Eastern Bureau, FLAG was able to plan all-important family gatherings in a less formal and more private manner than official Department briefings. At FLAG-sponsored gatherings, relatives could come to know each other better, be given information, exchange personal stories, and plan future activities to further a common goal. Emotionally beneficial as the Ops Center telephone system was, in the long run it took second place to FLAG, which provided the glue that held us together.

As days stretched into months, inevitably outsiders sought to exploit the hostage predicament. We needed legal counsel to dissociate ourselves from unwelcome nuisances: those who created hostage parlor games, T-shirts, and other items supposedly endorsed by family members for fund-raising purposes; then there were mysterious mailings of newsletters (patterned after our own) by unauthorized groups seeking publicity for their own causes. FLAG turned to Brice Clagett, a senior partner of Washington's prestigious law firm, Covington and Burling. With Covington and Burling's expert *pro bono* guidance, FLAG members also lobbied successfully on Capitol Hill for the Hostage Relief Act, legislation that among other things allowed for educational and tax benefits for hostages and their families. This Act was allowed to lapse before becoming permanent legislation.

At this writing, therefore, the appalling psychological costs of being a hostage are not compensated. In March 1986, however, the Omnibus Diplomatic Security and Anti-Terrorist Act passed the House. It provides that government employees held hostage will receive financial compensation for each day they spend in captivity. The amount will be determined by the world-wide per diem rate in effect at the time. Beyond meeting the needs of government employees, this legislation could provide a standard by which non-governmental organizations, including transportation companies, might frame their own compensation plans for employees, passengers, and others for whom they are responsible. All such organizations should focus on how to encourage support groups for families affected, provide psychological counseling, and meet all the other needs that international terrorism creates. At the very least, this would be a signal that the country cares for its citizens even if overriding policies must lengthen their confinement and prevent them from being returned to their families.

FLAG received help from many benefactors. Thanks to Lawrence Dalley, a Washington businessman, rent-free office space in downtown Washington was made available to us. A professional fund raiser volunteered his services to FLAG directors, who with his counsel were able to raise funds privately to pay for our own initiatives, office staff, and telephones. Several other Washington businessmen served on our advisory board, contributing valuable time to assist us where we lacked expertise. As hostage families we were constantly aware of the public support for the hostages and it was doubly heartening when so many private citizens volunteered their help in our day-to-day endeavors. From our independent office on Seventeenth Street NW, we were better able to coordinate our considerable daily work with the national and international media, assign family members to FLAG business and public appearances, and help reduce the enormous telephone bills each family was burdened with.

Although FLAG members were kept pretty well informed on a daily basis of what was going on through both government channels and wire services, certain government initiatives were never discussed with us. The most important, of course, was the rescue attempt of April 24–25, 1980. The raid happened to coincide with a FLAG initiative to send a small family delegation on a mission to Europe. We planned our schedule so as to attend the European Economic Community meetings in Luxembourg in the last week of April. Planning our itineraries and heading the delegation became my responsibility. President Carter discussed the trip with me and gave his wholehearted support to the enterprise. By then, the hostages had been in captivity for nearly two hundred days, a captivity for which the host government in Iran had accepted full responsibility. Our message to the people of Europe contained three major questions. First, was the takeover of our Embassy a problem concerning only Iran and the U.S.? The reality, we said, was that diplomacy and the concept of international law were being held hostage in Tehran. In that sense, the crisis spoke to the family of nations, who were in effect all being held hostage. The Iranian action could threaten relations and communications between all nations. Second, we asked: Could action by the allied nations make a difference? Iran has many historic and cultural ties with Western Europe: much of the Iranian leadership had been educated in European countries. We asked the people of Europe not to underestimate the impact of their actions on Iran. Third, we asked what would strong European action do, and answered the question ourselves: we felt it would dispel the growing fear that the alliances of nations are workable during "good times" and meaningless in times of crisis. Our appeal was not just to heads of state but to the families of Europe. "We are the hostage families of today; you may be the hostage families of tomorrow. We pray you will never have to bear the pain that we feel daily."

With guidance from the British, French, and German Embassies in Washington and with help from friends like Pierre Salinger, ABC's bureau chief in Paris, I firmed up meetings between members of our delegation and Giscard d'Estaing, President of France, Prime Minister Margaret Thatcher of Great Britain, the Most Reverend Robert Runcie, Archbishop of Canterbury, and Helmut Schmidt, Chancellor of West Germany. Besides myself, our delegation consisted of Pearl Golacinski, mother of Alan Golacinski, the captured Embassy security officer; Jeanne Queen, mother of Richard Queen, a young vice consul; and Barbara Rosen, whose husband, Barry, had been the Embassy press attaché. Ed Meyer, a correspondent from WMAL, a Washington ABC-affiliated radio station, and Tom Hanrahan of the New York *Daily News* accompanied us.

We had booked seats on TWA's 7:30 p.m. flight from Washington to Paris on Tuesday, April 22. That morning, Katherine realized that something highly secret was brewing. Chance observations led her to believe it might possibly be a rescue attempt. "Louisa," she said, "I think there's going to be a snatch!"

"While we're in Europe?" I gasped.

"I don't have any specific information," she said. "I just know that certain people are not in their offices . . ."

Stunned, but not wanting to alarm my fellow envoys unduly, I simply told them individually that if anything untoward took place while we were in Europe, we should go to an American Embassy and wait it out. Our schedule called for us to go to Paris together, meet with the French President, spend the night, and then on the following morning set out individually for London, Bonn, and Rome. We met with Valéry Giscard d'Estaing on Wednesday, April 23, the morning we arrived in Paris. He spent nearly an hour with us in the magnificent Elysée Palace while buckets of rain drenched the city and a mob of multilingual reporters waited for us on the slippery steps outside the ornate entrance. During our cordial meeting, Giscard d'Estaing locked eyes with me briefly—was he indicating that he suspected there might be an American rescue plan? He said nothing, of course. A day later, I had succeeded in putting this unthinkable possibility out of my mind.

On Thursday, April 24, in London, the possibility of a rescue attempt did not come up either with Mr. James Callaghan, leader of Britain's opposition party, or at Lambeth Palace during my meeting with Archbishop Runcie. Nor was the matter raised by Britain's Prime Minister during our conversation in her office at 10 Downing Street. But on two London call-in radio programs, one before and another after these meetings, a number of British subjects voiced their concern about such an American move. The widespread suspicion surprised me; I was so sure that such a plan, which naturally had been discussed early on, had sensibly been dropped, the problem in Tehran being very different from that at the airport at Entebbe, in Uganda, where a hostage rescue mission had been successful.

At 6:45 a.m. on Friday, April 25, the telephone rang in the apartment in Eccleston Square where I was staying with Sylvia Compton Miller, a London friend. It was a reporter from the BBC, who relayed to me the shocking news of the American fiasco in the Iranian desert and asked me numerous questions. At 7 a.m., Sylvia and I heard my answers on the radio, my voice trying to respond calmly. Listening open-mouthed to the BBC newscast, we learned no more than what the reporter had outlined to me fifteen minutes earlier. An hour later, I was at the American Embassy with Ambassador Kingman Brewster, who knew no more about the rescue attempt than I did. The only message the Embassy had received that day which bore any relation to the rescue mission was a classified telegram from Cyrus Vance to me regretting its failure and promising continued efforts on the part of the Administration to gain the release of the hostages. Because of the time difference between Washington and London, it was the middle of the night in Washington and President Carter had not yet addressed the American people. In Grosvenor Square, hundreds of newsmen had converged on the Embassy, and at 10 a.m. London time, Ambassador Brewster, still not informed of any details of the rescue attempt, asked me to field questions at a hastily arranged press conference. It was a tricky moment. The last thing I wanted to do was try to second-guess the President, who, we knew, was going to address the American public at 7 a.m. Washington time (1 p.m. London time). Since the raid was a fact and a failure, it seemed to me that my obligation was to play down the event and not fan tempers in Europe or Iran. When questioned by journalists at the Embassy that morning, I said I was sure that the rescue attempt had been undertaken as a mission of mercy and not with any military objective in mind. I said that I hoped the Iranians would not overreact, that they would not take out their anger on the hostages. And that I wished the rescue attempt had worked! There was little else I felt I could say. Subsequent radio, television, and newspaper interviews occupied me for the rest of this wearying day, until I was able to catch a night flight back to Paris. Sometime during the day, I spoke to Barbara Rosen in Bonn, who was as shocked and frightened as I was. She told me that our Embassy in Bonn had known no more than Embassy London about the rescue mission. She had spoken publicly in response to questions from the press, and her statements had echoed mine: the hope that the militants in Iran would not overreact. We shared the grief of the eight families of the men killed in the Iranian desert; their loss was greater than ours.

I contacted Katherine, in Washington, too. I was proud when she told me that the hostage families in the U.S. had taken a firm stand behind the President and had also voiced the wish that the attempt had succeeded.

I believe it was proper for the hostage families to take that stand. Our expressed loyalty to the President was the only way we had to help mitigate our government's incredible folly. For those of us who read and heard firsthand the adverse European reaction to the raid, this was hard to do. Even before the news, we had personally learned of the discomfiture of the European heads of state with the Carter Administration, which too often, according to some, went its own way without consulting its allies in advance on matters that concerned them. The Europeans saw the raid as more than a human tragedy. Looking to United States military strength for their security, they were appalled. Unfortunately, the deaths of eight airmen gave the Administration the excuse to present the event to the American people as a "tragedy," which implied that nobody was answerable, instead of acknowledging the sheer incompetence of the whole operation.

We continued as planned to the EEC meetings in Luxembourg to meet with officials of Belgium, Ireland, Italy, and other governments in our effort to increase European awareness of our very human problem. As a delegation we were well received, but we learned important lessons, too. President Carter had requested the nations of Europe to enact tough economic sanctions on Iran. In spite of their sympathy for the American hostages and their families, the Europeans did not support President Carter to the degree he requested. Only minor economic sanctions were imposed. On the heels of the takeover in Tehran, our European allies had all increased their shares of the Iranian market, which we had once dominated. They, far more than we, depend on Middle East oil. As an old Greek friend once reminded Mike and me years before in Athens: "The real question is survival." For most nations, economic considerations outweigh political problems engendered by assassinations or the taking of hostages. It is hard to know what will change this. In late 1985, after innocent travelers were killed or wounded by terrorist guns at airport ticket counters in Vienna and Rome, President Reagan's call for European sanctions against Libya met with similar resistance.

On the last day of our stay in Europe, our delegation had an audience with Pope John Paul II. Our few minutes in close conversation with him were not political in nature; those moments of being in a warm, loving presence restored a needed sense of hope and calm in each of us. The audience was well publicized and probably sent another signal to the Iranians of how little support they enjoyed around the world.

Back in the United States, we threw ourselves even more actively into FLAG. But as a result of the rescue attempt, we lost contact with the hostages. Letters stopped coming, and communication did not resume until late in the summer.

Our experience in Europe crystallized my views about the U.S. media. On the one hand, many of us welcomed their interest and the fact that they kept the hostage story before the American public—indeed, before the world. However, we did not appreciate network interviewers asking Iranian officials whether the Iranian authorities planned to try the hostages and execute them as spies. Such questions suggested that reporters were trying to push events to a climax, to create news. Confrontational questions like those tended to form stereotypes: simplistic images of good guys (us) and bad guys (the Iranians) which only fueled public outrage and frustration. Media hype seemed at times to undermine much of the

quiet diplomacy on the part of the U.S. and other governments and may just possibly have pressured the Administration into its decision to mount the ill-fated rescue attempt.
The dramatic day-to-day story of the captivity brought high
ratings to television news programs and boosted the careers
of a number of professionals in the industry. But, for all the
talent and money spent on the hostage crisis, the media only
infrequently scratched more than the surface. In no way did
they seek out and report that a powerful new Islamic political
force had emerged and that anti-American feeling is a reality
not confined to Iran. As the months dragged on, the networks
began inviting psychiatrists to appear on the morning shows.
These guests could very rarely shed any worthwhile insight
into our personal problems. Few such guests had ever had anything but secondhand experience with political prisoners, and
nearly all droned on about the Stockholm Syndrome as if that
particular condition applied to every hostage experience. What
became clear to us was that some of these doctors jumped at
the chance to be interviewed with a hostage family member
to further their professional careers. To my mind, what they
spouted half the time was hogwash, and I refused to participate when notified in advance that these so-called experts
were to appear with me. Nevertheless, the networks aired
their often half-baked conclusions with paralyzing regularity
in the last few months before the hostages were released, and
afterward: The American public was greatly misinformed.

Since my husband's return, we have together spoken to
many audiences about the nature of our crisis and how we
got through it. The main difference between our crisis and
"usual" crises we all go through is that ours became national
news. Our personal torment was aired by the world media and
shared by the American public. That the public cared was an
abiding tonic for us. The memory I most cherish other than
my husband's first telephone call from Wiesbaden, Germany,

after the hostages' release on January 20, 1981, was the seventeen-mile bus ride to West Point from Stewart Air Force base at Newburgh, New York, where the returning hostages landed. The license plates of the cars parked along the route of our motorcade made us aware that the cheering thousands had come from many states. The nationwide joy showered us—in the felicitous phrase of Katherine Koob (one of the two women hostages)—"like a bath of love." We saw old and young, family groups, Boy Scout troops, veterans in uniform waving banners and American flags; there were fire brigades and school bands. The tears shed were as spontaneous as ours. The television coverage that day surely couldn't fully convey that remarkable and emotional occasion shared by the former hostages, their families, and the American people. It was a moment of perfect happiness and mutual triumph that replaced thoughts of revenge, reprisals, and earlier reversals. I believe it could not have happened without all concerned having learned something about faithkeeping and personal growth. If we had to lose our privacy during the crisis and become symbols of a national nightmare to experience this overwhelming love, it had been worth it.

Our adjustment was complicated by the changes wrought in the hostages and in us who had stayed home. For example, I suddenly found myself no longer part of the news. The mantle passed to the former hostages. Now it was Mike's turn to rise with the birds to be off for hours at a time on talk shows and newscasts. My work in the State Department and at FLAG was over, and I missed it. Being a media spokesperson for FLAG had been taxing—sometimes interviews seemed to follow each other day and night—but it had become in a sense a job. My responsibilities put me in touch with many interesting people and new fields of knowledge. I was thankful that the crisis had ended, goodness knows, but having no further contribution to make left a tremendous void. Such a feeling of letdown is common after crises, which make a tremendous demand on us, and then, after they have passed, we wake up not quite knowing what to do with our changed selves. Adjusting takes effort and time.

Fame is a tyrant, hard and expensive to deal with. A blizzard of mail descended on the State Department (which delivered it to the FLAG office) and on every former hostage's home. Our weary postman made me think of Santa Claus as every day he trudged to our front door under the weight of his mail sacks. Before long, letters and telegrams covered every surface of every room in our Washington house. The urge was to respond personally to each message, but that was impossible and we were left reeling with guilt and helplessness. Like it or not, we had become celebrities, a condition we also knew would set us apart from our Foreign Service colleagues, who are expected to maintain a low profile.

When the Department offered Mike a senior assignment in Brasília, the time came for some hard decisions on our part. For some time, Mike had been considering a mid-life career change. The opportunity does not come to everyone, nor is the transition easy. But he took the plunge, retired from the Foreign Service in August 1981, and we moved to New York City. We encountered extraordinary financial difficulties and a sense of stepping out into space and severing lifelines from the mother ship. Our Foreign Service life—a constantly mobile one that entails sudden geographic changes and demands the ability to adapt quickly to new surroundings and community involvements—had equipped us, even as it had prepared us in some measure for the hostage ordeal itself. One positive side to the new life we chose was that we could be near our family. Accepting a foreign assignment with the Service, however interesting, would have meant another lengthy separation for Mike from our sons as well as the older members of our family. His decision to leave the Service was difficult, but we felt that he had made the right choice.

And so, in our middle years, we started again. To do it required, we soon learned, the stamina of youth, and in the process we managed to regenerate some of that buoyancy. Our new life has become rejuvenating and exciting. During his ordeal, Mike faced death several times, and I faced the prospect of widowhood. We learned to confront these possibilities with boldness. We now recognize the goodnesses in our lives and we can deal with our difficulties with greater perspective. We are so very fortunate!

People frequently ask us whether we stay in touch with other former hostages and their families. This is not easy to do. Many of the former hostages have resumed their careers overseas. Families that I became so close to during the crisis are, of course, spread out across the country. And, understandably, the former hostages do not seek reunions. Thanks to FLAG, which still exists and is now housed in the home of its volunteer corresponding secretary (the wife of one of the former hostages), we know everyone's whereabouts. We did not dissolve FLAG, although after the release we were pressured to do so. We feel that its charter and seal may sometime be of use to another group.

At the close of Bill Keough's funeral service, we stepped out into a bitterly cold New England day. Freezing rain and icy, gusting winds, the first real thrust of winter, seemed to be appropriate weather for the sad occasion. Yet so much of Bill's philosophy and perspective filled our minds that in a way it helped dispel some of our sense of loss. Speaking of Bill, the homilist did not speak of life ended but of life everlasting, and of the effect our lives have on others. Bill's life had been worth living, and it remains for us to learn from his experiences and profit from them. The quality of his life, not its length, was what was important. Bill saw his life as part of a plan. Mike and I believe that to be part of the plan still allows the opportunity to make choices at certain forks in the road. By these choices we grow, we gain new dimensions. Bill and Katherine did. Mike and I have made choices, too. For Katherine and ourselves, there will be more. Our friends in their fifties are beginning to talk about last jobs, their last productive years. Katherine, Mike, and I, however, are completing our first five years as survivors, and looking forward to a new and different life.

March 1986